DUPED

By
Joni Bohne

WRITTEN FOR THOSE WHO CARE FOR THE OLD,

FOR THOSE WHO ARE OLD,

AND FOR THOSE WHO PLAN ON BECOMING OLD...

BY SOMEONE WHO *IS* OLD

978-1-09834-575-4 Paperback

978-1-09834-576-1 eBook

DEDICATED TO THE *OLD AT HEART*.

CONTENTS

Why	1
How	11
Genesis	23
Bert	49
Sam	61
Angie	79
Tammy and Sam	89
Jeff and God	94
No Sam	97
Theories and Lists	109
Donna	122
He's Back	130
Oh Deer, Dear!	143
Just Slip Out the Back, with Jack	177
Making Amends Meet	203
Sam and I and Joy and Me	211
Never Been Good at Higher Power Math	225
Charlotte Made Me Do It; Love Made Me Not.	230

Why

I stepped out of the shower, wet, naked, and caught a glance in our above-the-sink mirror. And then I screamed. No reason comes to mind why I would have eyed my naked self in that mirror on that day, considering I had not done so in half a decade, other than because it happened to be the day after my forty-fifth birthday and I had been ruminating on *old* and *fat*. My scream was not an I-see-Norman-Bates-standing-behind-me-with-a-knife kind of scream, but more in the category of an emboldened-mouse-just-ran-across-my-foot shriek. Either way, there was no Norman and no mouse, just one plain and simple truth with which to reckon—my nipple would no longer make the mirror cut even if I stood on my tiptoes. Granted, it was a relatively high-mount mirror and my hammer toes coupled with a resultant weak gastrocnemius precluded a fully extended tip-toe. But even at that, it was still a shock.

He knew the difference between my sprinting rodent and stabbing intruder alarms. After more than twenty-five years, you know these things. He sauntered in, shoeing away the fog, his decades-old wire rims steaming up, a bland "What's up?" on his shrinking lips—those lips that used to be so full. Over the years, his wasting facial muscles had morphed him into the image of his late father, which would have been fine if I had liked that bigoted dullard.

Malapropos as it may have been, I actually took time, then and there, dripping and screaming, to formulate a private query as to why his glasses steamed, blinding him, and yet this same steam would not perform its fogging magic on that merciless mirror that had audaciously reflected my gravity-ridden chest. But his coat and the fact that it was an unseasonably cold early fall in the north woods gave away the science behind that phenomenon. I just had to remember, in my future, to never, never look. Never.

I told him. He displayed no change of expression, and this about him had been starting to really irritate me. He slowly peeled off his specs, right to left, like he was about to use a hand lens to inspect a diamond, navigating to within a near-sighted range of the mirror. And then he announced, in that spice-less tone that had lately so matched his demeanor, "I could lower the mirror."

He didn't get it. *He probably thinks this has something to do with me wanting to be able to see my nipple in that mirror,* I thought, *like I was undertaking a visual check for nipple cancer.* The civil engineer in him viewed the fix in terms of inches, not hugs. How did our minds age into different orbits when twenty-five years ago—hell ten years ago—we were so in sync?

Or were we?

Perhaps I should have seen this coming, this methodical, pragmatic, pancake-flat, low-volume approach to things that didn't so much matter, and even to some that did, or at least, I thought did. Subscribing to the continuity theory (psychosocial) of aging, I have believed that our personalities don't change as we age; that is, we are who we always were, only more so.

Therefore, I should have seen this coming right from the get-go when, having just returned from our honeymoon, I spied his fragrance bottles neatly lined at the rear of his dresser top, in *alphabetical order*. He denied this, but do the math here: Aqua Velva, Aramis, Brut, Canoe, Drakkar, English Leather, Old Spice Musk. The chance of this being a coincidence was somewhere in the range of Powerball odds.

Moreover, I should have seen this coming when three months into our marriage I noticed that his half of the closet was organized as such: shirts, pants, jackets (the order in which he put them on) and also organized according to color, and not just color—goddammit, I freaked—but according to hue from pale to bright to dark within each general color category. *And*—I'm not finished—the overall colors of the shirts/pants/jackets were in the order black, blue, brown, green, red, white, and yellow— a*lphabetical* again, denied again. Fledgling young and hell-bent on nesting, I postulated that it was possible that some people do such things unconsciously. Like a guy I once dated added up the house address numbers on the Minneapolis streets down which we spent much of our then lives surfing for a parking space. When I asked why he was muttering numbers, he looked confused, and then surprised, that he was even doing this. It took me three dates to figure out what he was doing (there was never a fourth date) and the rest of my life to figure out why I attracted these abecedarian types or—oh my god, say it isn't so—was attracted to them?

When I asked the psych people at work about this alphabetizing conundrum, they came up empty, albeit with little effort, and so I rubbed the sand out of my newlywed eyes and wrote it off as quirky, even cute, something to laugh about with the girls. And that I did.

Now if those weren't enough clues to prevent me from being surprised during that post-birthday mirror encounter, how about the fact that he was the only person I have ever known who tightened his shoestrings at every pair of eyes, from the toes to the instep, *every time he put them on.* Even when he was going out to retrieve our dog who had just dug her way under the fence and into the road. Even when the rain was coming down 800-count percale and his new Ford minivan was in the driveway with its windows open. Even when he was madder than hell at me for deciding at the last minute that I was willing to pain through that sci-fi movie he so badly wanted to see.

But, being fair, he also should have seen "old me" coming when he long ago discovered that I even bothered to decode his wardrobe arrangement—I, whose closet looked like the racks of T.J. Max on Black Friday, at closing; I, who rarely sported footwear that required fastening; I, who owned more than seventy-five pairs of resale bib overalls. Alas, neither of us should have been surprised that we were aging into who we always were . . . only more so.

That said, what really should have surprised both of us was that we lasted, and moreover, that we loved lasting.

Yes, it must have been that birthday and the seemingly sudden metamorphoses of both our bodies and our relationship. But unlike caterpillars, we could not shed our exoskeletons; we could not molt. We had started going to seed from the outside in.

I spent the rest of that day in tortured pursuit of supporting data that might serve to jump-start my ego into the hovering denial that was working hard to become its friend: North to south, were my lids draped over my eyes like a scarf window valence? How many chins were in my profile? There were seven between my two grandmothers. Did my neck resemble a partially closed umbrella, and were my toenails opaque like my Busia's? I skipped over my torso—never my strong suit, even in youth, hence the bibs. There, thankfully, were some nos to those questions, and I still counted only the two chins I was born with. But that scant positive data was not enough to satisfy my ravenous inner defense.

And it also happened to be the birthday on which my daughter forgot to call until 10:45 PM (Central), the birthday during which I received an iron from my husband along with a "Well, you said the one you have is crap" (and we're talking the kind of iron you get at a pharmacy or gas station—not a bell or whistle in earshot), the birthday on which my son called at 10:52 PM after his sister reminded him, and only after she had received a call from her dad— Iron Man—at 10:44 to complain that neither of them had called. He must have checked the answering machine, because I did not bring up their dismissiveness. The placating eleventh hour calls only made it worse . . . if only I had been able to figure out what *it* was.

Ah yes, *that* birthday that marked the days—fifty-nine to be exact—since my last period, because my last period started on my husband's September 1st birthday, which I vividly recalled because I had walked out of the Italian restaurant with a marinara-colored stain on the back of my khaki skirt (I had alfredo), and my birthday is the 29th of October, and thirty days has September. Easy and in-my-face math to add up to fifty-nine. And I hadn't had sex in at least twice that interval (seriously decreased libido layered with MLB playoffs), and what that meant was that I would have to spread eagle, in stirrups, in front of a very good man who happened to have nose hairs long enough to wrap around a half-inch curling iron. Then, once I got past those proboscis hairs, which always made my nose itch throughout the exam, I'd have to deal with the dark advent leading up to the delivery of the results that would take me back to his office. And therein, my mind would attempt to distract itself with short-lived filler thoughts, such as whether all of his patients got itchy noses during their visits and what, if anything, he made of that coincidence.

Moreover, if that was the fuel, here be the kindling. At the dawn of that defining birthday, while reaching for an alcohol wipe in the pocket of my scrubs, I noticed that there were more wrinkles on my scrub than on our recently departed Shar Pei. Embarrassed in front of my adolescent patient, I proffered: "I guess I should have used an iron on this scrub." Her reply, which only added to my budding ger-ascophobia was, "What's an iron?"

That birthday. Yes, I do think *that* birthday was a big influence on the *why*.

Or, maybe *it* was brewing well before that iron birthday.

Yes, of course *it* was . . .

I was the baby of the family and eventually the only baby when my sister died of brain cancer in mid-life. My mother was quite old when they had me, old for having a baby, that is. She referred to me as their "surprise" until I got my period, and then, once she explained the whole process of a woman's reproductive cycle to me, she started adding the adjective "menopausal" to "surprise." I liked being her surprise, plain or peanut, especially because she spent every day of my life proving to me that their surprise was a blessing for which they were eternally grateful. But I eventually came to know that it was she and not they. As my sister and I had discussed days before she died, Dad loved us regular and Mom loved us special. We truly adored that woman.

Before I had children and before Dad died, I might have said I was as close to Dad as I was to Mom, maybe closer. For it was only later that I understood my mother's love, perhaps Oedipus being operative in that miscalc.

Mom held back so Dad didn't look bad by comparison—Dad who loved hard, not soft; Dad who loved sporadically, not consistently; Dad whose love was payment for goods received, goods in the form of good grades, good behavior, good effort. So, what eventually impressed me about Mom was how she managed to step out of that dynamic and let her love flow freely to us *while* making it happen that we still loved and felt loved by Dad. It was an intertwined, intricate love, helping us love him because she loved both him and us. My sister, I do believe, would have said the same. Ironic that both of us nurses could not put a finger to that pulse.

To meet her, you would think she was plain ole pie dough. But she was filo, ripe for the layering. Therefore, decoding her love chart came much tougher than decoding Iron Man's closet chart. I eventually aged to learn that, for Mom, it wasn't so important that we felt loved by her as much as that we felt loved by both of them. For she didn't just play *her* love note, she conducted the symphony of all who loved us. Without her, I now imagine, we might have grown up disliking the father we grew to love. Only much later in our relationship would I understand what a gift that was. And I know that was special because I know I couldn't do it.

So, at that very point in time, when my offspring were barely remembering that I had pleasantly surprised their grandparents on that October forty-five years earlier, my hero was rapidly dissolving into my universe—her body, mind, and spirit folding like stiffened egg whites into batter. And I had been watching, closely, and I had already started to miss her.

She said Dad was calling her. Nice thought, but emphysema was calling her. Dad, I was certain, was doing just fine without her, secondhand smoke-free for once in his lives.

When Busia lived and Mom could breathe, I was two generations away from a waltz with my winter, but the gap had acutely narrowed with Busia's passing. Anxiously, I began dreading how it would narrow even more, very soon, when Mom would sneak away. I would have shared my lungs with her if I could, but they said no.

I had been watching also at work, as never before. Professional practices that I had witnessed for twenty-five years now appeared different to me. Images started to come into focus, front and center, that previously I had not been able to see, like those 3D pictures you stare at wherein there is an image hidden within another picture, which eventually most people can see if they relax their stare long enough.

And so I became able to see a duped fool sitting in a "geri chair," where once there had been a "cute li'l old lady," after my peer arranged for a male nursing assistant from the second floor to present himself as a doctor to this older adult patient and order the once-upon-a-time-cute-li'l-old lady to take her pill. And she did.

Her heart-shaped face framed a pair of extra-large eyes cast over a short, flat nose. Two cavernous laugh lines flanked her stubby nose and eventually met her pursed mouth after a long journey south. I thought of ET when I first saw her. And her personality was just as charming, just as innocent as the gentle alien, on most days, but not that day.

As she turned her head to avoid our intentions, a set of matted dull grey and tangled locks, which probably had once been housed in a bun when she or someone else cared, begged for a comb while the rest of her begged for a hug. But we were focused on the pill.

And the image I had seen before I stared hard and long into that 3D scene, for over twenty-five years as a nurse, used to be one of all of us feeling proud of ourselves for our cunning accomplishment—she had taken the damn pill. But on that watershed anniversary of my parturition, what came into focus for me, instead, was the image of a drooling duped fool, and then suddenly her face was my face, and I felt ashamed for what we had done—oh so many times over—to so many faces that were not mine.

In that moment, the well-worn and often flippantly used phrase "I wouldn't wish this on anyone" came to mind, and while the intensity of the situation supported that sentiment, my evolving attitude did not. Antithetically, I most certainly *did* wish this duped woman's feelings on them. *Let her feeble, helpless, done-to, dependent, impotent, vulnerable, exposed, abashed, and humiliated feelings be theirs, God, for at least one moment in their young lives.*

Then, on that day, in that room, I became that deceived patient. Not just her face, but all of her. My heavily weighted limbs could not move. My mouth could move, but not in the directions I was telling it to move. My voice box was more of a reed, squeaking out slim sounds that my lips could not sculpt. And my head was the only part of me that listened to my brain, rotating left and right to avoid the spoon of applesauce that they believed disguised my pulverized heart pill.

I didn't want the pill because I didn't want to continue on as what was left of me. But they were hell-bent on saving my body even at the expense of my spirit when they paraded that young man into my room, wearing a woman's lab coat, pretending to be a doctor. And even though I knew, I gave in and took the damn pill, because I was spent and disgusted with how unaware they presumed me to be when I could not show them differently.

Feeling her emotional pain as I did, the thought crossed my mind that I was experiencing those very emotions that I had wished upon my peers, those feelings that, instead, were perhaps wished by someone or something upon me?

And so, while claiming this old woman's spirit as my own, I began to abhor, in advance, the caregivers who would one day treat my mother and me and thee this way. Visualizing me and Mom in this frame spurred a pivotal reponse within me, both personal and professional. I not only reacted to the nurse I was, but to my birthday that wasn't and to my cord about to be cut for a second time. I became driven to spare my professional peers, and others, the struggle of waiting decades, or maybe forever, to get their patients, their aging selves, or their aging loved ones into focus.

Furthermore, I remain ashamed to this day that it took her duped face, reflecting mine, atop a mid-life crisis, to finally spur me into reaction and eventually this action. Better late . . .

And so, I guess, that is pretty much *why*.

How

How? I would become the cute li'l old helpless lady. Well, maybe not so cute and not so little, but for real, old, and for *not* real, helpless.

That is, in those first days of my forty-sixth year, I decided that, sometime after retiring, I would feign incompetence secondary to dementia and I would take in all that happened to me for the purpose of writing this book, assuming I would live that long and be up to the task. And if God was on board with my plan, I decided, He would take care of that caveat.

In the meantime, I would watch and pay close attention like never before. I would take notes and collect stories from the old. I would study the behavior behind the decline of some old brains, how the falloff began and how it progressed; that is, I needed a script. I already had a head start on all of this, having been a nurse for twenty-five years by that time. However, my birthday epiphany had made me aware that those twenty-five years as a nurse were service years thwarted by selective attention. If you do not know what this clinical psych term means, I suggest you do an online search for "selective attention test in basketball video" and take the minute-long test. You will then understand the difference between my professional observations before, compared to after, my "iron" birthday. I'm guessing that your smart phone is next to you, so please do this now so this important point makes sense to you.

* * *

You're back. Did you count the passes accurately?

After decades of this concentrated watching (some might call it mindful watching, but that is a little too "om" for me), when the time was right (and I wasn't exactly sure what I meant by "when the time was right" when I first contemplated the project), I would orchestrate my slow decline from an early to an eventual moderate progressive mental disorder that would land me, voluntarily, in an assisted living facility. During my stay, I would take voracious notes that would become the research for this work—the work that I hoped would, some book later, make a difference.

When it came to predicting how my husband and children would deal with my mental deterioration, I took an agnostic position. Perhaps, I can finally admit, it was that I did not want to know, more than that I did not know. Our family had a history of taking care of our own for as far back as I had been told, and told, and told. This tradition had backfired for many of us over the decades, as in "They just put 'so and so' in a rest home, but we never do that—we take care of our own," and then the gnawing, stomach-burning guilt when those words ended up being said at our last family supper with our beloved elder who just could not be managed at home any longer.

So that was a promise, I had decided, that should never be made or requested, and a proclivity that just might prove problematic for my project. That is, applying the "Cat's in the Cradle" philosophy, in reverse, my family just might feel obligated to keep me home. Therefore, to cover that base, I made it clear to all three of them, verbally and in writing, that I wanted to be cared for in an institution should my body or mind fail me to the point of requiring ongoing assistance, and that the last thing I would ever want would be to burden them in their home and test their patience with me. I went as far as to end every conversation about this topic with, "Promise me you will carry out my wishes and not selfishly carry out your own." I was good. Damn good. In fact, this talent that surfaced for setting the stage for my plan gave me the confidence I needed to feel I could pull off this ruse when that "right time" came around.

Dealing with my friends and neighbors during the project would be easier to manage, I predicted. I saw this undertaking as having three tiers. The first included my close friends, only two, which by the time the project had started proper, was down to one, having lost Julia to a car accident in the same year as my husband's death. My remaining BFF could be kept at bay over my six-month institutionalized winter with merely a couple of check-in calls and a few emails with grandkid photo attachments, especially considering she and her hubby were happily preoccupied with their new condo in Florida.

The second rung included our social friends, those who invited us to their Super Bowl and new year parties and their children's weddings. This group had dwindled in correspondence considerably once I scaled down to half mast, apparently my lone, it-could-be-you-next face tending to suck the life out of their merriment. Most widows will tell you that they have experienced this pell-mell retreat of friends, if you care to ask them. But if you are a most people, you do not want to hear it. So many . . . become so busy . . . so fast. Accordingly, I figured that all I'd have to do would be to text out a trickle of regrets over the course of the project's tenure, pandering to their avoiders' guilt by claiming excitement in my life, and then hope that none of the hanging-by a-thread remaining few would run into my children, which was not likely, logistically speaking.

The final and furthest-from-my-heart group, I feared, would become my biggest challenge. These were the day-to-day run-into neighbors, the former co-workers, the church people, the acquaintances who cut my hair or cleaned my teeth or sold me fund-raising dough braids, Girl Scout cookies, and home-made soaps, the now-and-then constellation who would try to get me to adopt one of their bitch's puppies, to keep my poor, lonely self company. And in and among this group were the most worrisome of all, the stop-byers, those who could never be completely accounted for in any plan—humanitarians who might grow curious about why an (old) widow was never answering her door that was barricaded by undisturbed snow.

Now, of course, I could have just put the "touch of dementia" word out there and that I required assisted living, but then I would have a tough time undoing that insidious permeation, which would be like the proverbial "Don't think of an elephant" or a judge telling the jury to disregard a comment. And, in perfect stride with my aversion to aging, I was just not ready for that impression of me to be anyone's impression of me.

My solution was this: hire the son of my most nosey and gossipy neighbor to remove snow while I was on an "extended vacation in Florida," visiting my various friends who condo-ed there. Kathy was certain to pass the word, and if she missed any stoppers, my property would appear inhabited. Should the deceased neighbors ever run into my deceased children, they would likely chalk up my invention to their mother sparing herself embarrassment. Tier three solved.

I felt quite good about this friend plan until the thought crossed my mind that the ease in which I was able to "deal with" my friends might be a message about how close, or how many, my friends were not. Something to work on post project, I shelved, lest it be a short funeral procession.

Finally, there were my grandchildren to consider. Truly a tough think. I decided early that I did not want them visiting me at whatever facility I chose for the project. How could I face those pure hearts with a lie? Like yellow snow. So, here is what I came up with: Tell Andy and Bonnie that I was agreeing to live in an assisted living facility "for a while," as a trial, which was not unlike most of the minds of those who agreed to move into such places. It is how families get them to say yes. And so, I would explain to Andy and Bonnie that I did not want to tell the grandkids just yet, in case I was to return home. What they told them privately, I could not control, but at least this way, I would not be facing them, wherever I was, with deception spewing from my "Noni" lips. I asked them to tell their children that I was vacationing in Florida, and my wherever institutional room would be sure to contain a palm tree somewhere in it for a Skype backdrop. Still a lie, but a more palatable one, from my perspective. Bonnie and Andy agreed to this plan.

Let me guess what you are thinking at this point when you consider how my family would feel about my perceived mental decline, and how I could stand by and watch their pain, and how I could deceive my friends so: "Who does this?" Right? Well, here is my short answer to that question: who does this is someone who sees beyond herself and those who matter most for an opportunity that might allow many more to become sensitized to the emotional changes inherent in growing old, and in doing so, hopefully, create greater knowing, better caring. At least that is what I was telling myself; it was my story, and it was sticking to me. Besides, I rationalized, chances are my family would face this pain eventually when it came to my real decline. The difference was that, in this case, I would get a chance to gather data on this process with a clear and present mind, and hopefully share my observations professionally, with that same mind. How is that for rationalization?

And don't think that question hadn't kept me up nights from the age of forty-five to the project's start, when my mind was pregnant with this plan, as in, how these relationships would change once they found out what I had done. What if I did not like what I observed about how my family was responding to me when they thought I was not aware? Throughout the project, that fear reared its ugly head and became even repulsive with each act of spurious disorientation I perpetrated. But, alas, I consoled myself with my belief that it was not like *that* would have been a virgin experience for me, or them. That is, not unlike most families, we had weathered mutual disappointments in one another before, and survived. We could handle yet another, I reassured myself.

And how about this for comfort self-talk? I considered that, if and when I truly did experience a decline in my mental capacity, how lucky my family would be for getting a chance for a do over with experience behind them to do it better, especially after reading this book. I would have liked that chance with my parents, for no matter how hard I have tried to convince myself that I did my best with them and that no one could have done it better, there are weeds that pop up in the thickly seeded sod of that resounding narrative that cause me to find myself, in the wee hours of my nights, wishing I could go back, pull those weeds, and make some decisions all over again. My family will have that opportunity, I justified.

Finally, a humorous anecdote came to mind that, given the do-over opportunity, would they ever even believe I was, for real, in my end, declining? As in, would they dismiss it as "She's at it again"? This caboose of a thought made me smile when it finally surfaced at the end of my train of fears.

And the long answer to that question is this book.

* * *

My plan was relatively simple in design and included the fact that there would be only two other people who would be in the know about this project—my doctor and a lawyer. At one early point in my plans, the thought did occur to me to include my husband and maybe even my children, but when I considered that this model would require an ability on their part to act, I came to the quick conclusion that not one of them had the talent to pull off this con effectively. If you met them, you would agree.

Additionally, in that design, there would be the absence of their reactions to my decline to consider. That is, I would be seriously limiting my data collection if I chose that route. Sadly, very sadly, that decision became easier for me when my husband died four years before the planned start of the project. By the way, his name was Jeff.

I had a good relationship with my hairy-nosed MD, and I had the feeling he would participate if he felt he was legally protected. I did not ask him to get onboard until my sixty-ninth birthday when I was about ready to roll. I probably should have been asking him about my waning libido over the prior two decades, but at least I could get excited over *this*. By the way, the missed period turned out to be early menopause—dodged that bullet.

The only lawyer I knew was a family friend who handled my parents' estate, and he, being an estate planning lawyer, would not be the person I needed for my project. But I trusted him implicitly, so I believed that, if I asked him to refer an intellectual property lawyer, he would do his best to pick a good lawyer for me and that he'd be okay with not knowing why I needed such counsel. He did not disappoint.

Jack Spiewak was the attorney he recommended. At sixty-nine, I was probably only a few years younger, I surmised, than this man who displayed a striking resemblance to Andy Griffith, the actor who played my favorite TV personality. And it bolstered my confidence in this Sheriff-Andy-Taylor-look-alike attorney that Griffith also had played the TV criminal defense lawyer, Matlock, even though I never watched that show out of my loyalty to the character of Andy Taylor. It just never seemed right, especially since I fantasized in my youth about marrying Andy and becoming Opie's mom. I had no idea what I would do with Helen. But I *had* heard that the Matlock character was a great lawyer. Jack, however, wore a dark suit.

Health insurance became the all-important concern for my two partners in avoiding crime. By design, I did not have long-term care insurance, so that bill would be out-of-pocket and not an issue. I figured I could afford, financially and emotionally, to do this for six months. The health-care visits to the doctor leading up to and during my institutionalization would be problematic. Even though this would be a voluntary admission, the assisted living facility might wish to see records and lab tests. Certainly, my children would—should. The lawyer said we—Doc and me—would sign papers, a "notarized affidavit," that stated I was responsible for paying back all insurance claims after the project was completed. My doctor said he would perform my exam visits pro bono, save the insurance payouts in a designated account, and return the funds with interest—credit card rate interest (ouch)—at project's end. With my state of mind pretending to be compromised during the project, my daughter would be looking for those "This is not a bill" statements from the insurance company, so we decided we would have to go this route.

The cost of the lab tests that would be done to rule out other possible organic causes for my cognitive changes, and that would all turn out negative (I hoped), would also be refunded to the insurance company at project's end. Because there were no validated biomarkers for Alzheimer's disease, and diagnosis was based upon documenting mental decline in addition to lab tests that rule out any other possible organic causes, we would not have to worry about falsifying lab reports for that tentative diagnosis. A huge sigh of relief was heard coming from Dr. Chott when he heard "not falsifying lab results." All three of us would sign a detailed contract explaining the project and our specific responsibilities.

My medical records that contained documentation of my symptoms of early dementia *would* be falsified. "But not *really* falsified," Jack and I explained to Dr. Chott, because the good doctor would be merely recording what my children told him, albeit with full knowledge that the behavior was an act. Those nose hairs of his boogied with each deep sigh that was exhaled past them during this discussion, most likely as the vision of his fleeing medical license was dancing in his head. I had the feeling he comforted himself with the thought that he was months from retiring. Jack was reassuring that this is done all the time in undercover research work and that we would not be vulnerable to litigation.

Finally, all three of us would hold copies of these records, along with the contract. My copy of the records and contract would be stored in a safety deposit box. We agreed on a very reasonable retainer fee for each of these men and included a percentage of publishing royalties, should there be any. When I read royalties, I could not help smiling at the confidence these two men had in me, which I did not. It warmed my pen.

I felt guilty about asking the good doctor to do this because I knew his conscience gave him no choice. Many years earlier, my part-time firefighter, part-time logger, and part-time small-herd rancher father saved Doc's daughter from her burning car. The accident occurred during a north woods' blizzard on a day the bare-ly-a-woman nursing assistant was on her way to work after having planned to call in because of the storm. Doc would never forgive himself for his words to his daughter that night: "Health-care work-ers don't get snow days, darlin'." A dead deer and a downed utility pole later, she was unconscious in her car that was just about to ignite when my father came upon her on his way home from a house fire. My dad's strong arms handled the extraction like just another calf being pulled out of its mother. Dad was unaware until after the save that she was the daughter of our family doctor, and Doc would never let him forget that she was. In fact, I half-expected him, at project's end, to say, "Even?" But the half of me that did not expect him to say that knew that a man like Doc would never equate a life with a piece of work.

I named Jack as my durable power of attorney for health care (DPAHC). This would preclude Bonnie, or much less likely Andy, from extending my contract at Borealis without my permission. Not that either of them would do that, I told myself, and yet I signed, probably a result of seeing all too many families in my career not acting like families should, especially under stress.

If this fact was leaked to them somehow, I would tell Andy and Bonnie that I did not want to choose between the two of them for the DPAHC role, that I wanted their input to be equal, and that I had chosen Jack accordingly to bring them together for every important decision.

Andy and Bonnie would buy that rationale because they had lived through the family horror of how Jeff's cousin, having taken the DPAHC role as if she had inherited the Crown, reigned over their family's kingdom and left her two brothers out of all decision-making. She had taken control of her mother's finances. She insisted on their mother living alone in her home despite the fragile woman's desire to move into assisted living. She threatened her mother that she would not visit her in any "home," nor would her children. She claimed her reason for rejecting such a move was that she "would never do that to her mother." That would have been believable if she treated her mother well, but she was emotionally abusive. The old woman was too afraid of her daughter to fight back or accept help from her sons. Truth was that the daughter did not want her mother's house to be used to pay for assisted living because she knew she would be inheriting the house. To be fair to the judgment of Jeff's aunt for her decision to will the house solely to this woman, it should be mentioned that her daughter *had* been quite close and very caring to their mother years earlier, hundreds of cases of wine earlier. In the end, the whole mess had broken up their family, and as a result, Andy and Bonnie had heard Jeff say more than once that he would never pick one child. I would simply slip in as an extension of that tenet.

Dr. Chott would be sure to tell them that this type of decision was not unusual for an older adult who was relocating to an institution, that the impending loss of control often causes the person to grab for any and all control left to grab. He was not wrong about that; he was simply wrong about that being me.

The staff would write us off as just another dysfunctional family who needed a lawyer to assume a role that healthy families doled out from within.

Signing those papers became the hardest task of my life, this thought thronging my mind: *Oh God, will my children ever forgive me? Will YOU ever forgive me?*

Genesis

In the beginning . . . there was Christmas in June.

"Hi Mom, what's up?"

"Hi Bon. Is this a good time to talk?" I had always asked that question at the start of our calls, but I became aware during that phone conversation that I never really waited for a reply Note to self: must work on that when this is over. It is amazing what you can pick up when you are concentrating on what you are saying.

I started with our usual chit-chat; we rarely got to our points without it. "Hey, I heard on the news that your school finally hired a new president. 'Bout time."

"Right?"

She had embraced the latest lingo fad of asking "Right?" when anyone said something with which she agreed, often interrupting, instead of the way it used to be when the commenter said it themselves, for confirmation, or no one said it. I found myself obsessed with counting her "Right?"s whenever we conversed, and during one conversation she topped out at seventeen in a period of ten minutes.

That day, I thought she was probably preoccupied while we were on the phone—I heard clinking and clanking and a lot of "Right?"s punctuating my statements. This reminded me of the

Deputy Warren character from the *Andy Griffith Show* whose trademark was repeated questioning followed by a rapid-fire succession of "Huh?"s.

I found this to be a terrible distraction and even somewhat of an irritant when communicating with Bonnie and so many others in and around her generation, which would not have been so bad if at the same time I wasn't being blinded by rhinestones on denim asses that were far too big to sparkle. Say, "Right?"

I admit that I had been tempted to hop on the "Right?" train, but eventually decided that, with an end of me in sight, why would I want to lose more of what was left of the real me? And then there was this: old people trying to act hip are often perceived as desperate, like "hot pants" long ago on our good-figured seventy-year-old neighbor—still hurt our eyes to look. Just not . . . *you know.*

She was up to eight "Right?"s on the subject of the new president, and while I had that number, solid, I hadn't a clue as to what she had said about the new guy. *When did this linguistic evolution take place?* I pondered, losing count. *Damnit.* Let's see . . . about the time "so" was replacing "well" or "uhm" as a sentence starter, and thong underwear peering above low-rise jeans like sanitary belts were about two decades gone. *Thank you, thank you, dear God for that.* Come to think, it was also about a decade after very pregnant women switched from roomy cotton maternity tops to belly tight knits that caused so many of us to fight the urge to poke our pointers into their Pillsbury dough boy bellies to check if those little turkeys were done. And their bulging umbilici, like perky cold nipples under wet t-shirts, made it that much harder for us to hold back.

I searched my generation's history of language and fashion for anything comparable, and all I could come up with was "Cool," which I had abandoned in late elementary along with pleated skirts with giant safety pins and go-go boots, having reasoned that, scientifically speaking, cool meant "not so hot," that the pins were fake (holding absolutely nothing together on those skirts) and that the boots were so cheap they hurt. I did, however, hang on to my Ben Casey blouse because I secretly wanted to be a doctor despite being told girls *had* to be nurses, or nuns, or secretaries, or "even better," stay-at-home moms.

The evolution of societal mores is difficult for every aging generation, but I contend it is especially troublesome for the Boomers to swallow because, having always represented the largest demographic, we have become accustomed to controlling consumerism. We also enjoyed command of the colloquial and are now relegated to dealing with a generational gap that conjures the image of Heston parting the Red Sea in Ten Commandments. And Metamucil and Benefiber do not quite make for the kind of *movement* that turns into trend. Just sayin'.

Back to Christmas, "Just wanted to know what time you are coming for Christmas dinner and if your exchange student—what's his name?—will be coming because I have Cornish hens and you know how that goes as far as the count," I said, and tossed in a "duh" chuckle for effect. The exchange student had returned to his homeland years ago.

Silence—a communication technique rarely used by either of us, stunned both of us into not knowing how to reboot. I reassured myself that I must have been effective.

Finally, "I'm sorry, Bonnie. What time did you say? I'm having trouble hearing lately. My right ear is still plugged from that cold I just got over."

"I'm having trouble hearing you too, Mom, *because the kids are so loud in the neighbor's pool*. What did you say, Mom?" Her speech pattern was slow and deliberate when she said the "because" part of that first sentence, typewriter speech. I imagined I heard a ding. She was working hard at re-orienting me to time. We live in northern Minnesota. I doubted that there were kids in an outdoor pool in early June, in the morning, on a school day (mega snow days to make up that year). Then again, maybe, she does not lie well. She lies a lot, about stupid stuff, but not well. I guess I did that too with my mom, a pick-your-battles defense mechanism that is built right into our DNA—a regret.

"Just asking who is coming for Christmas dinner and when, and also whether you are all staying overnight. I need to get my beds made with fresh linens. Well, I guess that depends on the weather, right? Oh, gotta go, honey. Timer just went off. My pecan lassies need to come out. I'm making them for Gordy; you know how he loves them. Last Christmas I swear he ate a whole dozen!"

Bonnie lived an hour away, and unless the weather would be horrendous during my imaginary Christmas, as in roads would have to be closed, her husband, Gordy—a closet smoker who always gets itchy and restless around the in-laws—would always have wanted to go home rather than stay overnight. The sugar from the pecan lassies helped to stave off the nicotine withdrawal when he was with us, and thus the lassies. And that corsage we mothers get on the day we become mothers-in-law ought to come with a case of Orajel— enough said.

"Mom, I'll be heading your way for a late meeting with the Courtney group. Why don't I just stop by and we can talk about it? *It's warm outside. Real warm.*" *Ding.* "Maybe take a break and put your feet up with a cold LaCroix. See you soon." *Click.*

It wasn't that warm. She was doing her best to reorient me out of December. I doubted that she had a meeting. I worried that she felt the need to leave work. She terminated the conversation before I could demonstrate I had straightened out mentally. I never expected her to visit. *Crap, now I have to make those cookies.*

I squirmed uncomfortably in my tangled web.

* * *

As I watched her approach my house, I knew she was not headed for any meeting. She wore dress-down Friday clothes, a style she would never sport when meeting up with the woman whom she squeaked past for the job she then held at the college. No make-up, and her hair was greasy, in a sloppy pony. Having inherited my waist, her short shirt did not quite climb over the small roll flowing over her too-tight jeans. Come to think of it, I thought, as I laid eyes on her shabby sneakers, she didn't even look good enough to have been at work on a Friday. Maybe I caught her on a mental health day off. Maybe she *really was* at home listening to some cold-weather-tough preschool or truant kids in the pool. And what a spoiler of that this would be, I sadly thought, for my fast-approaching daughter whose stride and eyes were wider than I had ever seen either.

Bonnie walked slowly through my back door, slightly crouched, reminding me of how Jeff looked when he would check our partially covered live trap, suspecting skunk.

She looked so worried, frightened. I didn't know whether she was afraid for me or afraid for herself; I recall those two types of fears blurring into one when I dealt with my mom's decline. I hated myself for even wondering which it was for Bonnie.

While I had been waiting for her to arrive, I imagined that Bonnie would expect to see me rocking in a fetal position with pics of long-ago Christmases strewn about like giant confetti. I hoped that she wasn't disappointed when she found me hanging curtains—I really did not want to have to make those cookies.

"Mom?" Her voice cracked a hair. She waited for a response, not just a verbal response, but a whole package response, needing an immediate clue to my state of mind.

"Oh my gosh. Hi Bonnie! What are *you* doing here?"

Her speechlessness, again so rare, so loud, was unplugging my for-real plugged ear. I hated that she was worried, not that she didn't do her share to keep me worried from the time she grew breasts until the time I lost one of mine. But I told myself that this was not about payback, and yet I wondered whether convincing her of that fact at project's end would be any harder than convincing myself.

I came down off the step stool, slowly, giving her time to make her assessment, and finally, when I was three feet from her and demanding nonverbally that she explain her presence, she calmly and tonelessly said, "Mom, I told you I was coming when we talked earlier." She was much better at this than I had anticipated.

"Oh, that's right. We did talk. You said you had a meeting and might stop. I guess I got so busy with these curtains that I lost track of that. Good that you are here, though, because it gives me a chance to stop this insanity. This rod is really too big for the head on these curtains."

Bonnie surveyed the kitchen for evidence of cookies in the making. "You said you were baking when you called." I was amazed at how sensitively she was going about this, not directly confronting me with my Christmas in June.

"I called *you?* Hmmm. Oh. Maybe. Baking? No, I wasn't baking. I will be, though. It's Karen's birthday tomorrow so I'm bringing a cake to bone builders. Maybe I'll throw in some calcium chews to fit the theme and offset the sugar." Bonnie chuckled, and she was not a chuckler. She was a squeaker when something was just a little funny. She obviously was shaken, poor thing. She displayed her "I'm going to puke" look that I well recognized from Christmas eve, midnight mass, 1983. But this time her stomach held strong.

Bonnie took a long look at me, and then an even longer look around the room. She eyed my parka on the deer antler rack next to the back door, the coat that I had dug out of the crawlspace and hung there just before she had arrived, for effect. She eyed the postal letters on my dining room table that I scurried to set up right after I planted the coat—three envelopes, two of which were sealed, stamped, and addressed to friends, one laying open as bait to set the stage. More about the reason behind that later. Bonnie bit: "What's with all the mail, Mom?" I was quite certain she was thinking that I was writing Christmas cards to go with my Christmas-in-June invention. She looked relieved when I told her I was just writing friends, keeping up. "Me-mail," I added, "my personal campaign of writing to people in long hand with no acronyms, no keyboard, no emojis."

Other than the coat, which she could have reasoned might have been left over from our cold spring, Bonnie came up short on evidence of my mental incapacity, and she gave up. And that is one big difference between Bonnie and me: I would not have given up, but then again, I am a nurse and Bonnie is a guidance counselor at a state university. She, more than I, recognizes the value in being able to let things go, she who loses 20 percent of her students before the start of each new semester, and an additional 30 percent by midterm. Bonnie obviously had concluded that this episode of mine was transient and therefore was not giving it a second thought. That was fine with me. The seed was planted. Goal met.

"Coffee?"

"Sure."

I moved close to her and gave her the welcome hug I still owed her. "Bonnie, this is such a nice surprise, a midweek visit! No coffee an', but I do have some killer ice cream—orange sherbet and vanilla ice cream with a hint, just a hint, of clove. It makes a cup of coffee stand up and take notice." I was back to my usual self and she was off the scent of my decaying brain, texting, probably her husband or her brother, or both, with her follow-up report. And very soon she also seemed close to her usual, talking about herself, and I wondered if I might still work off what was left of her quickly dissipating mood of concern to get her to hang those curtains.

* * *

Here are some highlights of more of my Christmases in June.

On July 2, I pretended to forget Bonnie's birthday—a first. Okay, maybe that was a little payback for the iron birthday decades ago. I admit that I have a little get-even streak in me that I have always attributed to being pummeled as the baby of both my immediate and extended families.

On July 4, at a fireworks display, having not returned from the porta-potty, Andy found me directing traffic in the parking lot. My explanation: "I am service oriented." In fact, I had provided that same service at least twice before in my life, when traffic lights were non-functional during snowstorms, and both times I was reprimanded by the police when they finally arrived, in one case as much as an hour later. One would think they would thank me for all those accidents I prevented. This, however, was a little different—there were no traffic lights, no storms, and teenagers with flashlights were assigned parking and traffic duty. But my traffic-directing experience explains why this role came easy for me.

In early August, I called Bonnie to ask her how to get home from church, telling her the construction signs confused me. Church was a mile-and-a-half from my home of thirty years, and there was no construction.

In mid-August, when Bonnie, for whom I was dog-sitting, came to pick up her boxer and asked what was wrong with her dog who was listless after having vomited the remains of a desiccated ground squirrel, I told her that I had left Zoe, wearing a bark collar, in the utility room for a whole day, forgetting I had a dog in the house. I impressed myself when I came up with that story, extemporaneously, as I did.

In late August, I drove away from a gas station in someone else's white car; mine was red.

In early September, I told a close friend of Bonnie's, who recognized me in a hair salon waiting area, that I had six grandchildren (I had four), pretending to use confabulation to cover up not remembering their names. I used the names of the Brady Bunch kids. I happened to know this woman was going to a craft show with Bonnie that weekend; the incident would be reported.

In mid-September, I showed up braless in a tight see-through blouse at a university concert in which Bonnie was singing—talking 36D here. I don't think anyone except Bonnie really noticed because I carried my jacket strategically when out of Bonnie's sight. But Bonnie very much noticed, and when she introduced me to her choirmaster, she had the same look I once had when at ten years old she told her friend, within earshot of the friend's mother, that I had said her thong underwear peeking out of her low-risers looked like a sanitary belt on a plumber's butt. Bonnie was too old to be excused for such behavior, I was mortified, and those thongs, again, would be blamed for zapping the strength out of my polite.

I must admit—I enjoyed playing both the traffic cop and bra-less concert-goer scenes. And that really should not have been the case, and it continues to worry me.

That same week, Bonnie visited, which she had been doing much more frequently, and she found me wearing Jeff's sport coat and pants, claiming I thought they were mine. Jeff was 6'4"; I am 5'5". Two days later, with Bonnie at close range, I was not surprised to find myself visiting my nose-haired project partner, Dr. Chott. And it was easy to not smile because I felt very dirty, and I wondered if he did too when we heard the tremor in Bonnie's voice.

Oh God, help her to forgive me . . .

I felt hypocritical invoking God for favors when for most of my adult life I had been espousing my disbelief in intercessory prayer. My reasons for the rejection of this practice were threefold: First, my prayers were never answered the way I wanted them answered. Second, I believed that God already knew what we wanted and needed, so what was the point? And lastly, if I believed in these request prayers, then I would have to believe that someone with a lot of people praying for them was more likely to get God's attention than some poor unfortunate who had no one, and well, I just wouldn't want a relationship with the likes of such a higher power. I did not merely abandon intercessory prayer cold turkey, however; I asked around. I asked ministers, pastors, priests, a rabbi, and a Buddhist monk. They all seemed to give me a version of the same answer—God wants to hear us ask. Now, I had trouble with that answer because, again being that baby of the family, this smacked of God doing a pin-down and demanding that I say "Uncle." Perhaps I overthink.

So why, I asked myself, was I rooting to this beseeching behavior after so many years of denying its value? And I couldn't just turn it off—these prayers kept popping into my head, uninvited. After significant rumination on this phenomenon, I concluded that guilt had paved a road for desperate to travel, and this road led me to intercessory prayer. A "just in case," spiritual insurance, perhaps inherent in our design, eh God?

* * *

Bonnie gave me my granddaughter Helyn's bedroom for my birthday. It was tough leaving my home. Even though self-induced, this glimpse into my possible future caused me to worry whether the entire project would be a painful foreshadowing. That thought was beginning to haunt me. The day after my move, I handed over my car keys to Bonnie, having flunked Dr. Chott's mental acuity exam, or passed it, depending on the owner of that perspective.

He told Bonnie that he was prescribing a generic form of a what he called a "brain drug." In fact, it was a generic form of my blood pressure pill that I had been taking for years. Dr. Chott gave her what he called "samples" in a bottle. Now, a health-care-savvy daughter would have questioned that presentation. Not to worry with Bonnie. Dr. Chott had been Bonnie's doctor for all her life, and she trusted him with her life, her children's, and mine, but perhaps, once she learns, nevermore, I daymared. That said, for once in our lives together, I was grateful that she was not detailed-oriented.

Oh God, please help her to forgive him . . .

The plan was for me to develop subjective adverse effects, namely headache and nausea, from my brain drug, with no improvement in my cognition, and then he would have to try another drug. I was restricted, of course, to subjective adverse effects (headache, dizziness, nausea, flashing lights) because, by definition, these could not be validated by another person, as could an objective effect such as vomiting. I was good, but not that good. I considered slugging a dose of ipecac, but decided headache and nausea would do the trick—no need for overkill, considering the last time I had vomited was the day after my mastectomy and the mere thought of it still caused a shot of sting in my well-healed incision.

The next drug would be a generic form of my thyroid pills that I had been taking since I was nineteen—more samples. There would be subjective adverse effects of that second brain drug as well—flashing lights and vertigo, in addition to no improvement—and at that time I would start to display unsafe behaviors. Doc would tell us to dispose of the meds, and I would make sure Bonnie did that. I would start back on my trade name thyroid and blood pressure pills. I would have been taking fake (harmless supplements) labeled as thyroid and blood pressure pills during the fake brain-drug trials. These tablets did not have any little letters and numbers on them, but we both knew Bonnie wasn't going to catch that.

Dr. Chott's ability to deceive and seemingly enjoy this role began to frighten me at times, until I thought about who I was and, well, what could I say about that?

At one point, he said to me that he wouldn't be messing with my drugs like this if I weren't a nurse, and a smart nurse at that. I teased back that I wouldn't be asking him to if I weren't a nurse, and a smart nurse at that. We trusted each other, and that made all of it okay for both of us.

Eventually, the ruse proceeding as planned, Doc recommended to Andy, Bonnie, and me either around-the-clock supervision in the form of a live-in caregiver or institutional placement. At that time, I was portraying that phase of progressive dementia wherein I had long coherent and normal stretches punctuated by short spurts of bizarre, disturbing episodes.

So, at least once a week, I made sure to ask a question, the answer to which I should well have known. For example, to Andy, at my move-in birthday party, I asked: "Where is it you and your family live?" To Bonnie, I asked: "Oh, you work outside the home? Where?"

The periods of lucidity afforded me the window necessary to coherently reinforce my desire to be institutionalized rather than be cared for in either of their homes, or in my home with a caregiver, and to justify (to them) not putting up a fuss about eventually giving up home and keys. Recall, I claimed to be service-oriented—I aimed to please. If I were a dog, I would be a Lab. I acted as though I believed what they were telling me about my behavior and that it scared me into cooperating, as unusual as that would be for someone with new-onset dementia, but they were none the wiser. My compliance was necessary to move the project along.

Except for the me-mail letters, which I continued to write with increasing frequency, and which I began storing in easy view (and never mailing), I became reclusive from my friends. I did this for two reasons: first, this is a common development during the stage when one realizes their brain is not functioning well (avoiding embarrassment), and second, many of my friends were nurses and their expertise could present problems if they started asking too many questions, especially regarding my treatment plan.

God, I won't even ask you to help my friends to forgive me.

As the plan unfolded to the point of discussion of my institu-tionalization, I again struggled seriously with aborting the plan, at least that part of the plan that involved deceiving my children. But as I pictured the admission process, specifically the interview of my family, I knew they could and would not pull it off if they knew. My goal was to feel what it felt like, in my family, and in one of the best assisted living facilities in the Midwest, to be a person whose brain was not predictable. Again, their realistic reactions would contribute greatly to the project. Therefore, I decided, with much trepidation, to continue as planned.

To ease my conscience about exposing our family interactions, I decided not to identify all the specific reactions of my family, as such, in this book. My family could eventually be identified, and this would be all too personal to reveal. So, I recorded their reactions in my notes, and these reactions appear interspersed among the accounts I detailed about my observations during my institutional-ization, reactions towards me and others like me—well, others like fake me, that is. Therefore, the research was not lost; rather, it was transposed, to protect my family.

What I *will* say about their reactions is that, soon after I had moved in with Bonnie, both she and Andy were convinced that I was experiencing mental decline, but up to that point, it had been transient and benign. They appeared—I could not believe it—more charmed than worried, by what I gathered they considered to be "cute" confusion. I heard through the bathroom vent the word "harmless," accompanied by chuckles and comments that added up to cute. I hated that they appeared unaffected, almost amused by my waning. I know I should have been relieved, considering my con, or I should have at least given credence to the likelihood of there being a defense mechanism buried in there somewhere that the two of them were synchronously using, but instead I was hurt. That aside, I was not going anywhere in that state. I had to become unsafe. And their dismissive take of me made the planning of unsafe that much easier for me.

Accordingly, on Halloween, just as Bonnie pulled into the driveway of her ("our") home, I turned up the burner under a simmering pot of popcorn and oil, all the way to high. By the time she got in the house, I was pretending to be asleep in a lounge chair while flames were raging in the pot that was filled to the brim with popcorn and oil. I was going to make popcorn balls for the trick-or-treaters, a long-held family tradition (but only after I had made sure that the fire extinguisher was in its proper place and that it was functional).

When I fake-awoke to a frazzled Bonnie, pretending to not remember her name, I knew I would be giving up Helyn's room soon. And, I could not believe I had done this.

Bonnie arranged to take the next two days off from work, and a temporary caregiver arrived a day-and-a-half later—cute little thing from Malaysia who treated me like I was a toddler. Eventually, I would spend Thanksgiving with a whole bunch of people I did not know in a place called Borealis.

* * *

Oh, she was so careful not to call it a nursing home, the word "nursing" catching on Bonnie's lips like termites on an aardvark's tongue. It was a "nu—senior living residence," a "nu—assisted living center," and a "nu—senior community." And our tour was a "visit." And my room was a "suite." There are blogs entitled "semantics of senior living" that suggest all the right words to get mom or dad to agree to these places. She must have done her homework, and without me hounding her. She *had* grown up.

We, Bonnie and I, visited four not-a-nursing-home homes, and I had nothing but good things to say about all of those facilities because it served my project to do so, as in I had to get Bonnie and Andy to agree to one of these "communities." But that is not to say I was not tempted to have some negative say. My children probably liked me with fake dementia—I was so much easier with which to deal.

We chose Borealis Senior Living, an assisted living facility about halfway between Bonnie and Andy, close to two hours from each. I guessed that Bonnie was up for an equal-opportunity role reversal, for a change, as in making it easier for Andy to share the burden . . . of me.

I voted for Borealis for several reasons: I was assured a private room since all of the rooms were private, it was reasonably priced compared to others in its class, it came with a Polish cook (pierogis and kolacky were her specialties), there was no "memory care unit," which meant I would be living among residents with varying degrees of both mild physical and mental deficits, and finally and most importantly, I liked their answer when I asked if I could miss breakfast if I stayed up late and woke up late.

When I asked about missing breakfast at the other places we visited, I pretty much heard the same response: "We would prefer that you would try to get on our schedule for meals." But the Borealis representative/tour guide said with a wink, "Sure, as long as you don't expect to be served a hot breakfast when you eventually do wake up." Over the course of our married tenure, Jeff and I owned three fishing boats, and all displayed the same name, "Crack o' 10:00." Point, Borealis.

As an assisted living facility or a "residential care community," no direct nursing or medical care was provided at Borealis. Because there was no specialized memory care unit, persons who required closer monitoring owing to advanced stages of dementia, or "neuro-cognitive disorders" as the "tour guide" called it when we were touring, were not "candidates" for Borealis. And, for current residents for whom this eventually became their fate, she whispered loudly to Bonnie that the resident would have to transfer to a skilled nursing facility that could better meet their special needs. Coincidentally, Borealis just happened to be the main feeder residence for a skilled nursing facility that was a convenient quarter mile down the road and that they part-owned—well-planned. Emphasizing the word "policy," she made this canon copiously clear, almost at every hallway turn, claiming lack of space as the reason behind the "policy." I picked up that this word and her emphasis of the word worried Bonnie, but it was not like us for her to initiate that conversation with me nor me with her. Naturally, I was not concerned about this caveat, counting on the fact that my measured faux decline would not put their "policy" to any test.

After the tour, we were taken to visit with the Borealis intake coordinator, aka "rental agent." This middle-aged woman, who wore a whole lot of cologne, make-up, scarves, and very little fat, offered the Borealis synonym for forgetful as "age-associated memory impairment or AAMI." Her favorite color was definitely, most definitely, cyan, down to the little fish that swam in her little office tank. As I eyed her surveying my bibs, her remote smile and crossed hands made me think that Da Vinci had met her in one of her former lives.

I most surely had met her before—she was my statistics prof, my father's proctologist, and St. Mary's mothers' club president. I tried hard to like her, and eventually I would be successful, but not that day. I searched for a pic of a dog or a kid to help make that happen and finding none, I settled for distracting myself from her bristly persona by counting scarves.

During this meeting, or interview, as the scarf lady called it, Bonnie described me as "forgetful." I had been aiming for, and therefore would have labeled my behavior as "mild cognitive impairment (MCI). AAMI refers to a normal decline in memory due to aging. MCI refers to a more advanced decline in memory that may indicate the early stages of dementia. One distinction offered by some experts is that, in AAMI, the person will eventually recall the object or situation they have forgotten, but in MCI, this is "less likely" to occur. But the definitions of all these terms are replete with "may" s and "could" s and "possible" s and "less likely" s and "more likely" s, which, in the end, leaves the whole assessment process to be a crap shoot of sorts. And so, one person's AAMI becomes another person's MCI, a virtual cauldron of alphabet soup.

My reason for aiming "higher" on that scale, or lower if talking about cognitive function, was to assure I got placed. With Borealis, it served their purpose to use the AAMI definition because Borealis did not "do" too far into progressive dementia. Bonnie wisely left out the popcorn incident during the "intake interview," having figured out from the website and the tour that, for Borealis, there is a narrow, grey distinction between "forgetfulness" and "dementia" on the mental decline spectrum, namely safety, and so Bonnie was careful to describe me on the forgetful, safe end of that continuum. She claimed that the reason for my placement was "merely" that I was having difficulty keeping up with home management, my "mild, occasional forgetfulness" again merely adding to the home management issues.

Andy was obviously taken aback by this misrepresentation, shooting Bonnie that well-traveled brotherly look that begged for her to take the high road and be forthcoming. Apparently, they had not talked over this presentation, likely because it may have been an extemporaneous adjustment Bonnie had made as the Borealis "policies" started to more deeply sink in during the tour. Compliantly, I was able to reinforce Bonnie's spin when I artfully became the simple yet clear-minded tourist who followed my children's lead like a waddling duckling. I made sure that I looked and acted like Bonnie was describing me, like I was Borealis-worthy.

As a nurse, I need to be clear here that certainly all persons who experience forgetfulness do not eventually experience dementia. There are statistics about that transition that I will spare both you and me as these numbers about these issues, which raise with age, scare me, because, frankly, I am, these days, raising exponentially with age. After sixty-five, we are talking a helium balloon. That said, it is true that people who experience dementia experience forgetfulness first, hence the continuum.

After the tour, when back in her office for further information and Q & A, I noticed that the "very nice lady," as Bonnie later referred to the scarf lady, made eye contact with me only when specifically talking about an ADL (activity of daily living) that I would be expected to participate in, such as meals. But even then, she did not address me completely; she addressed me with eye contact, but her words addressed Bonnie. So, it was, looking at me, "Your mother will have choices of two meat entrees and at least three hot vegetables at both lunch and dinner." Otherwise, she limited her eye contact to Bonnie, having given up on reigning in Andy, who had his eyes fixed on me the whole time. And when she did make eye contact with me, she cocked her head and arched forward, leaning her chest on her folded arms that rested on her knees, like she was passing a hard stool. I saw myself addressing my grandchildren and decided then and there never to do that again. When she spoke to Bonnie, however, her spine was straight and perpendicular to her hips. Height was not the issue; Bonnie and I were still the same height, thanks to genes, calcium, and yoga.

* * *

I must admit—the room was not bad. It had a North woodsy feel, and I half-expected to look out and see a waterpark and glacier-carved sandstone formation or two. Even though I had a private room, I scoured the walls and ceiling for a camera, knowing that would not be the case but I could not help it. There were fresh flowers in the room on the day I "moved in." Never, never, never say "admitted." On the pillow was a tiny box of Frango mints—I had thought those died with Field's.

My Borealis closet included a laminate chest of drawers topped with a shoe rack—odd—and a rod for hanging. There was also a dearth of flat surface in the room. One small, short, very heavy table was located nowhere near either of the two outlets. One of the outlets was located inches under a narrow shelf that hung inches under a wall mirror. For phone chargers and a doll's hair dryer? And there was a small secretary desk accompanied by a laminate chair that obviously did not match it. I didn't check, but I had the feeling that there were outlets under one or more of the wall hangings—keeping them up to code, but out of reach by the preponderance of us with limited reach. Lighting was exclusively overhead.

The rationale behind the motif intrigued me. Perhaps nowhere to put or plug in contraband, such as hotpots, candles? Definitely not Feng Shui. Later I would learn there was a fire. I had the thought that

I would have to charge my laptop on the easily moved sore-thumb chair or get a strong arm to move that table, and I had the feeling it would be moved back lickety-split. Until I remembered that I didn't bring my laptop, couldn't bring it, for fear of blowing cover.

This was my first experience with being protected from myself since I was a child, and even though I understood, I felt restricted, juvenile, parented. It triggered an uneasiness that caused me to question my plan of staying six months. *Buyer's remorse*, I consoled myself. *It will get easier. It will be okay.*

I quickly filled my small dresser/closet with bib overalls (only twelve pairs), leggings, Columbia Henleys and long sleeve tees, thermal underwear for jammies, Vibram toe shoes, and Mukluks and Bean wool socks (should they ever let us out in the snow). The bibs have always been more of a comfort than fashion statement, having done the math on my waist to hip ratio decades earlier, which easily calculated to one. Hence, if it fit good on my waist, it was baggy in the butt, and if it fit my butt, I could barely breathe for the constriction placed on my descending diaphragm with each breath I took. Jeff thought the bibs "unsexy" and so I had backed off them, yet barely a day had gone by since he died that I did not wear them. *You're welcome, Jeff.* Bringing only twelve was a significant stressor because I could not decide which were worthy of the cut. They held memories and were more than just comfortable—they were a comfort.

On move-in day, I checked out the attire of my fellow community members—I would not fit in. I decided I would need to have Bonnie bring me some regular "elder" (during our initial visit, that's what the rental agent called us) clothes because I felt it was very important to my project that I fit in. I was baffled as to how I had missed this in my plan. Perhaps because I was so focused on the medical aspect. Elastic waist pants and pastel sweatshirts with animal and plant appliques and screen prints would soon be on their way to my closet. And sneakers. Because all I had to do was tell Bonnie I wanted more comfortable and easier to manage clothes, "like hers and hers and hers." *And forgive me God*, but I thought it would be amusing to catch that "look" Bonnie would shoot, which she thought I was not catching, in response to that request. It worked; an eyeroll later, I was being told she would stop by on the weekend with "comfy" clothes.

Bonnie brought me two sweatshirts, the kind with white fake collars that make you think there is a shirt underneath: one white with birdhouses on it and the other periwinkle blue with birch trees and chickadees. I know you've seen them. My favorite color is yellow, but at least she remembered no pink. The elastic waist pants made me cringe but, admittedly, proved much easier to manage in the restroom compared to bibs. I would eventually wear these clothes for a week and then abandon the fashion fit-in effort. For starters, the sweatshirts were too warm in a place where the heat was jacked up to compensate for the warmth that could no longer be delivered to so many bodies with sclerosed blood vessels and weakened hearts. And I just could not think in clothes that were not me. They would have to take me as is.

I came with a glut of stationery supplies, and I started writing within the hour of my arrival. I was writing letters to someone, and letters to no one, letters that were legible, and letters that were not, letters that made sense, and letters that did not, and letters containing an assortment of all the above. Letters, letters, letters. Dr. Chott, per our plan, told Bonnie, who then told the not-a-nursing-home staff, that writing letters was a stress reliever for me, that in a world that I could no longer make complete sense of, this made sense because I had always expressed myself best in writing.

Truth was I had strategized that, after watching me write non-stop and nonsensically for weeks, no staffer would be too interested should they find me writing in my room at night. And there would always be a cover page or two of the bizarre stuff on my clipboard. Dr. Chott added that I was not to be discouraged from this activity and these letters should be treated as my private personal space, read only by others when I requested them to do so. I loved that man.

That did not stop me from being careful. I kept my notes in a secret, locked compartment of my suitcase. I bought this suitcase around the time I had the idea for this project, at a 103-year-old woman's estate sale. Under a faux bottom was a secret base compartment that could be locked. I kept my fake writing props in the upper unlocked section of the suitcase so that the image of me foraging through my luggage was a familiar sight to all. I kept my project notes locked in the secret spot under the faux bottom. And I cannot, 'til this day, open that suitcase without wondering what the original centenarian owner of the case had been hiding. It smelled like money to me, but perhaps that was my wild imagination at play. Her name was Lola—that just added to the invention.

Despite the heads-up from Dr. Chott, it still became common for staffers and residents to use my writing to make conversation: "What are you writing today, Joni?" My response was always, "Me-mail." Bonnie translated that response to the staff and ironically "me-mail" became a household word in a place that no one dared call a "home."

And I never thought I would ever say this, but I missed my computer terribly.

I was relatively quiet at Borealis, quiet for the first time in my life. Poor Jeff missed this. I decided I needed to be subdued in order to do my concentrated watching and listening. And I did not want my personality to influence the happenings around me—I have tended to lead conversations. The proverbial fly on all those beige walls was who I wanted to be, other than my timely displays of forgetfulness that punctuated my otherwise unobtrusiveness.

Besides my quietness having served to make all who knew me come to believe that there were indeed personality changes accompanying my forgetfulness, there was my unremitting compliance that was so not me. There was reason for this too, and it was simply and importantly to spare my children having to deal with my resistance to being placed in a "nu—senior center," in addition to them having to deal with what was happening to me, especially when it wasn't really happening to me.

Accordingly, I planned to make it possible for my children to tell themselves, and anyone who would listen, that it appeared to them that I liked Borealis more than living alone at home. I would have to move gradually on this scam with Andy, though. Adult Andy has always read me more accurately than adult Bonnie, simply because he has always paid more attention. Consequently, he would not be so easily convinced that I was happy in my new home, as would pull-the-blanket-over-her-head Bonnie who would jump at any available opportunity to be relieved of the guilt of placing me.

Andy looked like me—fair, fighting fat, fine hair. And he acted like Jeff—persevering, peacekeeping, palpable (barely). The first time he visited me at Borealis, Andy came alone, on my fifth day in my new "residence." I would learn later that he had solicited help for the timing and the decision to come solo. I love him so much for caring enough to seek that counsel. And he didn't play games. He said upfront: "Ruth wanted to come but I wanted to visit you alone, first." And I understood why. Ruth, and even Bonnie for that matter, would have tried their best to convince him that everything was fine, even if it wasn't, and he wanted to make that assessment without escorts. That was Andy.

From early on, Andy adjusted to life's bumps differently, probably better, than Bonnie, because truth was something he did not hide from—Andy faced, whereas Bonnie effaced. And what Andy faces, he organizes. He has always been a tallyman, keeping account and then summing up. He owns a comic book shop, the irony of which is that he had never even touched a comic book before he owned that shop. His friend, Jimmer, owned the shop, and when Jimmer learned he was facing a fast-approaching cancerous death sentence, he put in his will that he wanted Andy to buy the well-established business from his mother, his sole heir, for what Jimmer had paid for it some fifteen years earlier. By then, it was worth a lot more. This was a complete surprise to Andy at the reading of the will, Jimmer having never mentioned this plan to Andy. But Andy understood that his friend had been playing the don't-ask-lest-he-say-no-card smack dab alongside the he-can't-deny-his-dead-friend's-request card.

Andy was a good friend. He knew what the shop meant to Jimmer and that he had been chosen because he had business and money acumen. Jimmer did not want his business to fold at the hands of some comic book junkie who overextended his or her (likely his) credit, thinking it would be heaven on earth to be able to read comic books all day long and make money at the same time. In a nutshell, that was kind of who Jimmer was before Andy got him straightened out business-wise. They were friends since they lined their toes along the property line that separated their grandparents' summer homes, where each boy to man met during summer vacations. There was the only place Jimmer did not bring his comic books. His grandmother would not allow it.

Jimmer left Andy some guidelines, about ten hand-written pages worth, to get him through knowing nothing about the comic book industry. Among my favorites were "Never tell a customer or any person who might come in contact with your customers that you did not spend your life reading comic books," "When in view of customers, handle the books like they are sacred, presenting the books to the customer like they are a crown on a pillow, for a king," "Turn book pages carefully, like you are peeling the backing off of cheap contact paper," and, "When you don't know something about a series, say 'wasn't a fan but I'll find out.' These customers respect purists, Andy." You gotta love a friend like that.

Andy did the math and decided to leave his job at H&R Block and continue to do taxes, independently, behind the store counter while waiting for people to buy his comic books, and, later, his base-ball cards (a huge fan) and other collectibles. By the third year, Andy was pulling in six figures. Go figure—a total *marvel.*

So, I was quite certain that Andy would do the math, as well, on me, and therefore I had to be prepared. I told him I liked it at Borealis and while it wasn't home, at least I wasn't lonely. I told him I had made quite a few "friends" in the five days I had been there (only staff by that point), and I made sure he saw that. "Being nurses, we connected," I told him. His side glances were making me nervous, but before leaving he said, "I was worried about how I would find you, Mom, but you actually seem okay, like not only okay on the outside, but okay on this Borealis inside."

Providentially, I added up for him, bless his ever-loving (count them, Andy) four-chambered heart.

Bert

A couple of weeks in, I still had not made any friends among the residents—probably my quietness, I reasoned. I did have a nice chat one morning with one interesting woman, Giselle, who said she was a precious gems dealer turned philanthropist. I *wanted* to believe her. She seemed to know a lot about precious gems, but then who was I to evaluate her expertise when I knew as much about gems as Andy had known about comic books. She did look the part, however, colorful stones adorning her ears, neck, and all her fingers. But whether they were precious to anyone beyond herself . . . no clue.

The philanthropy element was especially interesting to me. She claimed she had personally funded, or solicited funding for, over two hundred surgical relief tours to Central America for cleft lip and palette repairs in children. She said that the incidence of this condition was 1 in 700 in this population. Her story was that she was traveling on a private plane to South America for the purpose of buying gems when she became aware that the pilot was drunk. She ordered him to land the plane immediately, which he did, in a rural farm field. From here, Giselle set off on foot, in three-inch platform sandals, to the nearest sign of civilization, which happened to be a two-room thatch-roofed adobe hut in Honduras.

While trying to communicate to the five-and-a-half home dwellers about her need to get to the Tegucigalpa airport, using hand gestures and drawing with a stick on their dirt floor, she noticed a pair of small bare feet peeking from under a corner-hanging curtain. As she communicated her desire for an explanation of the hidden person attached to those feet, the feet began slowly disappearing from her sight. Curious, she persisted, only to learn that the family was hiding a girl of no more than four who had both a cleft lip and palette. She soon learned that children with this birth defect were kept from the rest of society, allowed no interactions outside the family—no school, no church, no friends.

It was then, she said, that she decided to put her gems to better use and fund a series of surgical relief tours to correct this problem. After her first few tours, almost 100 percent of the expenses were covered by donations and volunteers, including professional staff services, travel expenses, and supplies. Hundreds of repairs were accomplished during each four-day tour.

She could not have made this up, I thought, realizing by then what it took to make up even commonplace happenings. This had the sound of real, but then again, I thought about where I was and who I was not, and doubts creeped in, incrementally, with each point she seemed to be trying too hard to make.

I did pick up one gem from Giselle; some, apparently a combination of staff and residents, nicknamed our abode "Boring-all-of-us." One would have thought Borealis might have seen that coming, and if not that, then how about the fact that Borealis, short for Aurora Borealis, describes a phenomenon of colliding charged particles. And weren't we just all of that, I soon discovered. I decided I would not join the rebels and would continue to call my home "Borealis."

After our exchange, Giselle returned to her room, and I was scavenging in the day room for a potential friend, or more honestly, for some research material. Some called it the "day room." Some called it the "community room." My guess was that either there was an intentional switch to community room that hadn't yet completely caught on, or perhaps transplant staffers from other facilities had integrated the name from their former employ. Community room seemed more logical to me because there wasn't a night room. And I don't know why I used up so much energy thinking through such inconsequential incongruencies, but I had been doing that more and more since living at Borealis.

On that late morning, in that room, there was a tangible buzz of excitement. Staffers were standing along the walls of the large space, in pairs, talking quietly while looking towards the south end of the room. There, two staffers were kneeling at each side of a seated resident named Bert. She—yes, she—whose name was short for Bertrun, was Borealis' quietest resident, even quieter than I was acting. Quiet of voice and quiet of presence. Bert clearly sought out company, however, unobtrusively showing up everywhere, at activities, celebrations, meetings, meals. But she blended in, rarely a word, never even a nonverbal cue worth trying to interpret. Up until that afternoon, the most interesting thing about Bert for me was her name, and even that was not solely about her, for her late husband's name was Ernie. And the staff and residents got mileage out of that.

Bert lived a simple, low-profile, unassuming life at Borealis. She was the resident who, if she died and her body was removed during the night, no one would ever ask about her, no one would ever miss her, unless they happened to channel surf through a Sesame Street episode.

In a word, Bert's appearance would be described as "dull." She obviously cut her own hair; from the side, her locks resembled a bar graph of stock market activity in a volatile quarter. She wore grey clothes (not necessarily their original color), grey hair, a grey complexion, and out of cloudy grey eyes she looked anywhere but at anyone. I had the feeling her soul pitched a matching hue. Bert was a woman who clearly was no longer living for herself, luster-lacking and likely faded from all the wear and tear on what perhaps was once color-rich and even bold in her life.

So, it was all of Bert's grey gloom coupled with her fixed careworn expression that curiously contrasted the flanking, kneeling staffers who sported half-smiles and smirks. What was going on? I had to know. From a nurse's perspective, Bert looked okay, so I didn't think she was sick or hurt or that they were bringing her bad news. More closely surveying the staffers along the wall, I saw cats with canary feathers sprouting from their mouths.

To solve this mystery, I had to work the staff, and perhaps a few residents, who appeared to be in the Borealis loop. I had been edging my way into that loop, identifying those who would eventually facilitate my entry. It was not tightly knit; there was room. Within a few hours, I took pride in getting to the bottom of that community room scene.

Here's what went down: Earlier that day, Bert solicited a kitchen worker to pose as her doctor when contacting her three children to tell them that their mother was very sick and would likely be dead within forty-eight hours, and that they should drop everything and come soon, very soon. I could not begin to imagine Bert conveying all that information or taking such initiative. The kitchen staffer, whose fear of losing his job wisely trumped his temptation for the two hundred dollars cash-in-hand that Bert offered him for the task, reported Bert's request to the nurse. The nurse then notified both Bert's doctor and her durable-power-of-attorney-for-health-care daughter, only to find out that this was Bert's "second crack at this type of stunt."

Collating the beans spilled by Bert's daughter, her doctor, and the staff, I deduced that ten years prior Bert had run a similar sting when she paid $1,000 to a total stranger, a man she solicited during a Thanksgiving Day Parade, to call her three progenies and pose as a sheriff who was delivering information that their mother had died. Well, not a total stranger, if one considers he was "Santa" in the parade. Per Bert's direction, the jolly ole elf also told them to be at Bert's home at a specific time, where they would meet the funeral home director and Bert's lawyer for the reading of their mother's will.

The Santa sheriff further stressed that the meeting needed to take place *before* funeral arrangements were made because their mother's last will and testament contained detailed instructions regarding her internment, instructions that involved them, and upon which the will was contingent. Furthermore, he warned, Bert had specified that attendance of the meeting was required for any of them to be considered an heir. Bert reportedly had written out the actor's script and was standing next to her hire during the call, ensuring that her investment was well spent.

The fact that the Borealis "rental agent" was married to the brother of Bert's doctor made the filling in of all the details easy as whipped cream being piped into puffed pastry shells. I imagined Bert's doctor sharing Bert's first attempt during some family gathering, drink in hand, coarsely exposing the idiosyncrasies of his patient population. He probably rationalized that he hadn't used her name, but he *had* used her spirit and that was just as bad. It made me sick to think of it. And I was just starting to like the scarf lady.

In that earlier decade, a younger, quicker-thinking Bert probably believed she had thought of everything necessary to bring her three children together, those offspring who had been completely estranged from each other, and virtually estranged from their widowed mother, except for greeting cards for all those Hallmark moments. The split had occurred shortly after Ernie's death when the children learned that their father had left his half-million-dollar summer home to only their daughter. At her husband's funeral, Bert explained to her children that she was as surprised as any of them to learn that her name was not on that title. Her daughter claimed the same. Her sons weren't buying either of those claims, even when they learned that Ernie had owned the property well before his marriage to their mother, basing their distrust on their sister's abrupt cozying up to their father from the very moment she heard the words "poor prognosis." Litigation later, they would find it wasn't quite that simple, but in the process of that discovery, family ties were severed.

Therefore, when the "sheriff's" call came, one son, steeped in suspicion, smelled a rat, and called the real sheriff's office for validation. He did not bother to notify his siblings of the fraud, nice brother that he was not. The meeting between the much-alive Bert and two of her three children ended in a battle the likes from which even Custer would surely have retreated. And once again, the real sheriff got a call, this time to temper domestic violence.

At the end of that drama, Bert's daughter would forever resent her brothers' charge of financial exploitation, and Bert would spend her days at Borealis wondering what she did to deserve that Sinterklaas stuffing her stocking with three pieces of hardened combustible rock.

It made sense to all the Borealis staff, in defense of Bert's choice of methodology, that the way to get sparring people together was to use what split them apart in the first place, as bait. In the case of Bert's family, that was money. But the element missing in that equation was trust. Bert had not accounted for that detail.

I knew only three things about Bert before that day, the first being she and her husband's fluky Sesame Street connection, the second that she liked potatoes, and I knew that because during the few times I had occasion to eat at the same table as Bert, the only words she uttered were "Potatoes, please." And the third thing I knew about her was that she liked "*Little House on the Prairie,*" because at three each afternoon in the community room she would meekly call out "*Little House*" when others were calling for *Judge Judy, Wheel of Fortune,* or *Decades.* She was never heard, or perhaps just never acknowledged. I was never sure which.

Now it wasn't clear to me whether the fact that Bert ended up in Borealis by the following Easter had anything to do with her Thanksgiving reunion efforts, for apparently until that late morning of her second shot at securing a *Little House* family, those in the know had kept her secret from the rest at Borealis. But it was no longer a secret. *And now,* I then contemplated, I knew more about Bert than she wanted me or anyone to know, more than we had a right to know. So much for HIPAA (Health Insurance Portability and Accountability Act), and as the writers of that regulation probably sleep soundly, basking themselves in the denial that keeps them believing that their law about protecting patient privacy was a success, Bert's secret was being exposed to the staff and the likes of me. And people whose names she probably didn't even know were voyeuristically claiming her private dysfunctional life as theirs and enjoying it. I was sick to death of myself for ever delving. And I remain sorry to this day, Bert.

Among the staff, Bert became an overnight celebrity. "You go, girl" and requests for high-fives were among the many line drives that Bert had to field, without a mitt. The eyes of staffers and a handful of residents sparkled as they began vicariously plugging their own families into Bert's sting, wondering if it might work in their worlds. And during this flurry, I could not help noticing that the health-care workers at Borealis appeared to have a high incidence of family dysfunction.

If Bert was aware of the collective rumination on her undertaking, she did not let on. She so reminded me of the "duped" old woman who was responsible for me being at Borealis. I sadly could not recall that woman's name, but she came up so often in my thoughts that I decided then and there to name her. I chose the name Charlotte, not for any discernable reason; the name just popped into my head when I pictured her, or maybe I just remembered.

Bert had Charlotte's same vacant stare, but if you looked more closely, there was a depth in those eyes that you knew housed a lot of *know*. And looking at Bert, I pondered that, before I had met Charlotte, I would have been limited to seeing only Bert's vacant stare, missing that which spoke behind it. Before Charlotte, I would have joined ranks with the march of staffers, echoing their "at-a-girl" mantra, in synchronized cadence, like she had scored points, intentionally, for mothers everywhere. But Charlotte taught me to sense the soul behind that shroud of Bert's emptiness, so that on that day, I finally came to see clearly—thank you Charlotte—that Bert had not done this to show or show up anyone.

She hurts, I thought. And the child abuse slogan, "It shouldn't hurt to be a child," came to mind. I looked at this woman whose face displayed the road map to her private hell and thought: *Who should it hurt to be? Bert? What had she done or not done to deserve this, other than perhaps age beyond the years of being that child who should not hurt?*

The next evening, when the celebrity factor had worn off, I saw Bert in the community room. I sat next to her, my clasped hands on the table between us. Her head hung low, like so many heads did at Borealis, whether heavy from so many weakened muscles or heavy with so many years of disappointment, or both. Without extending her neck, Bert rotated it very slowly and looked up at me, expecting another one-liner, I supposed. I said nothing. After a few quiet minutes, she placed her hands on the table, one very close to one of mine.

And I thought, these four hands had prepared meals for, and changed diapers of, and held hands with, our collective children, perhaps even at the very same time and with the very same sentiment, yet then, on that table, only inches apart, these foyers of affection were coming up empty for both of us, for perhaps very different reasons, but nonetheless, equally empty. I ever so slowly pulled mine apart, covering her awaiting hand with the warmer one of mine. After several minutes of silence, our flesh fused as one, her neck swiveled even further for a better glance, and I gave her a slow nod.

My nod shook loose the pendant teardrop that was hanging from my right lower lid, and, after it fell onto my forearm and before it quickly absorbed into my timeworn dry skin, Bert noticed, and muttered, "I just wanted us all to be together."

It was in silence that she had heard my voice. And all I could think was that, for all my career, I had missed so much of real life, real nursing, *by talking.*

* * *

I got friends. The clothes probably helped.

I started talking a little more and a little slower. I learned that, when one does not talk in such places, the assumption is that they can't. And when one talks fast, well they don't, hence the need for me to slow down to maintain my cover. Slowing my talk was especially difficult for me; I was—am—a fast talker.

The plan to increase my talking made me nervous because it reminded me of trying to come off from a successful diet and attempting to eat moderately. Never happened. Food was an all or none. Either I ate too much, as in gaining weight, or I ate too little, as in losing weight. And so too, I feared, talking would be the same way, and that once I started, I wouldn't be able to stop. Apparently, food and voice, for me, are controlled by a toggle switch, not a dial.

I decided to record everything I said to people when out and about during my day and then count my words (there's where Andy gets that trait) in order to make sure that my talking was not getting out of hand. I really missed my laptop here, where I could count on Word to count my words. I did my morning tally after lunch, which was "quiet time"—never say "nap time" —and again after dinner, easy for me to not be missed during popular toileting time. My first day of counting, wherein I made a considerable effort to restrain my conversation, I considered to be my baseline. My goal was to say no more than 20 percent, give or take, above this baseline. Furthermore, if I couldn't recall all that I had said, I would cut my verbal output drastically the next day because not being able to recall so soon after was probably, I decided, proof that I had said too much to remember.

When I tried this method during dieting, listing everything I ate, it was effective for a while but never quite caught on as a habit. But it was all the idea I had for tempering a behavior, so I went with it.

This word-tallying also disciplined me to journal twice in the daytime, instead of leaving all my recording for the evening. The late-night journaling had been working fairly well, except for the vigilance of one nice night-shift staffer who niggled me about getting to sleep. She went about it so sweetly, albeit as persistent as a hungry house fly, popping in on the half hour like a bird in a clock: "Would you like a back massage?" "How about some warm milk?" "Maybe if I read to you?" Finally, one night, frustrated, I accepted the massage, the milk, and the reading session, and then made damn sure I stayed up all night, interrupting her with my many requests. And that was the end of the nice night nurse (I think she was a nurse; her ID badge was always flipped, and she never said) trying to get me to sleep. I liked that she tried, though; I would like to think I would have done the same. And I worried that I might become the reason why she would quit trying with other residents who were *over*-cover, unlike me.

I started to like it there. The food wasn't bad—there was even salt and real butter in it. And I was loving that I had no household duties except to make my bed, and once I even left it unmade to see what would happen, and someone made it without mention. But to be fair to the many people who did not like it there, some saying loudly so all could hear, some mumbling their discontent as if they feared the staff would retaliate if they heard, and some saying so non-verbally, their message falling on deaf eyes, I fully understood that it was different for me because I had chosen to be there, and with just a phone call to my lawyer, or perhaps either of my children, I could be on my way home within a matter of hours. That freedom made not being home so much more tolerable, not unlike so many of our southern slaves, I came to imagine, who made the decision to stay with their former owners once they were free. Freedom, the salve that takes the sting out of staying where you'd rather not be.

Not surprisingly, a major concern of the residents at Borealis centered around what was happening to their homes and in their homes, and what was happening to their pets. We did not get a pet after our Shar Pei died—for me, because of this project, and for Jeff, because of me saying we needed our freedom, not to mention that the dog had left a painfully lasting taste of loss. I love dogs, and so I felt the residents' dog-owner pain. No one cares for a pet like the ones who love it and the ones who love it first.

My house was a concern for me also, but not in the way it was for my friends at Borealis. Jack (Matlock) took care that my house could not be sold or inhabited while I was away; he had me put himself as executor of my will. When the project was over, he would take himself off as executor, as per our written contract. It was not that I thought Bonnie or Andy would try, but Jack suggested this move would give me peace of mind.

Bonnie and Andy would never know, unless of course they "tried," but the fact that I agreed with Jack regarding this arrangement worried me about myself. It seemed to me I should have countered, in a heartbeat, "That won't be necessary." We sometimes think we know who we are, until we are tested.

But I *did* worry about freezing pipes and windstorm damage. Alas, I was beginning to fit in at the "nu—senior center" in more ways than just my clothes.

Sam

The first *real* friend I made at Borealis—real in the sense of being a resident with whom I could relate—was Sam. I think he became my friend because I was the only resident awake when he had his spells. Thus, we noticed each other. Well, I noticed him consciously, and he probably noticed me subconsciously, in the wee hours of the morning when he lived out every "elder's" nightmare—becoming the *why* of there. He was labeled a "sundowner." By day, he was a handsome man in his early eighties (looked a lot like Ronald Reagan) who could play a mean game of cribbage, yet by night he was a wild man, arms flailing, yelling, crying. The first time I witnessed one of his nightly episodes, I was surprised he was allowed to stay.

He was playing solitaire in the community room when I first approached him. "Like some competition?"

"Depends. What-a-ye play?"

Now I came from a gamey family; we played cards daily (only three television channels), the loser giving the winner a back massage or taking the winner's turn at dishes. Being the youngest by eight years, expectedly I was the loser for most of those years. But I wanted to compete, despite the odds. Accordingly, I became proficient at massages, dishes, and eventually cards, all kinds of cards. My sister would surf a ragged Hoyle book for different games whenever I started winning. Took me years to figure out her conspire; my parents were forever unaware. But as luck would have it, by the time I got good at playing all kinds of card games, my sister left for nursing school, and the card playing all but stopped. And I was *so* ready.

However, at Borealis, being unsure of Sam's ability in a place where ability dragged behind it a question mark rather than a period, I aimed for simple. "Rummy?"

He smiled, a rising right corner smile that helped his right eye to half-wink. A pearly grey penumbra around his corneas reflected the overhead light, appearing halo-like. Called arcus senilis, these hazy gray half-circles, made up of lipid deposits, are common in older adults, especially males—I didn't have one of those…yet. And then he said in a low mellow voice, "Might as well play Old Maid." He tried another wink, his dry eye holding the working lid down for longer than a wink should take. I identified with the desiccation of formerly moist body parts, water shifting in our aging bodies from where it used to be to where it should not be, and I just knew that he, like me, hated when that happened.

Now here I go ruminating on the derisory, but, as a towering, once-upon-a-time strapping' guy from Wisconsin (the Packer's sweater gave away that he was a cheddar head), it struck me as odd that he would reference Old Maid, rather than Go Fish. Perhaps, more the effect, I reasoned.

We settled on cribbage per his suggestion. I always fancied myself as an above-average cribbage player, mostly because I was able to beat Jeff, 80 percent of the time. And I know it's not fair to say something like that when the person is too dead to defend his record, and, in fact, summoning honesty, that record might be a tad inflated owing to the fact that all I had to do was turn on the television while we were playing and it would distract Jeff enough for me to catch an edge. It did not matter what it was, but usually it was Pandora (classic rock), and he could not help but try to guess the song and artist. But even at that, I felt justified because a large part of any game is knowing your opponent's weakness, is it not? Now you say, "Right?"

Sam, however, I soon found out, was in a whole other league when it came to cribbage. He was masterful, a player who kept track of cards he buried in the crib and wisely applied this knowledge during the play, a player who remembered every card his opponent showed early during play and from that extrapolated the remains of their hand. I had been a player who relied more on luck than skill and often did not bother to give a hooey beyond the five cards I was holding, but Sam's challenge *(sorry, Jeff)* caused me to up my game. Lord knows there was enough going on in the community room to distract Sam most days, if nothing else, the blaring television, but he maintained his focus. If he had Alzheimer's, like I heard a couple of the paraprofessional staff suggest he had during his walks on the wild side, I wanted it.

He was a Paul Simon fan and he often hummed his songs, usually, "Still Crazy After All These Years" and "50 Ways to Leave Your Lover," but as luck would have it, it only made him sharper at his game. Occasionally, after melding high, he would turn over the count to me with, "Make a new plan, Stan." And I would shoot back, "No need to be coy, Roy." I put in a request for "The Boxer," thinking I could distract him with my "lie-la-lie" chant and percussionist impersonation to the tune of a biblical forty count of cymbal crashes, but alas, came to find he was a purist—no Garfunkel. There was no shaking him; he was a rock, and I wondered if he was also an island.

One game, I summoned the nerve to ask Sam, in an ever-so-calculated clinical tone, if he remembered what had happened the night before, referring to one of his nightly bouts. His face flushed, and he lowered his head as he mumbled, "No." He must have been told about these episodes of agitation, I thought. His face looked so not-Sam that I abandoned further pursuit and felt bad about asking in the first place, especially when I ended up winning that game. He obviously did not see me as a nurse, at least his nurse, even though he knew I had been one for over forty years.

Sam's troubling disturbances rarely missed a night, and when I would hear Sam out there in the echoing hallway, I would come out of my room and act as if I was just responding to all the noise, as if I didn't know what it was, and I would watch. He was a tall man, so all hands were on deck, leaving no one with the time or the will to pay any attention to me. Every night, the staffers talked calmly to Sam, tried to distract him, and then led him back to his room. I overheard that Sam's daughter, holding the durable power of attorney for Sam's health care, refused for her father to have any form of sedation, "day or night," so chemical restraint was out of the question—but probably only, I thought, until he hurt someone. I was surprised as well as glad that Borealis included this night-time escort service in their assisted living package. They liked Sam, and so did I. So Borealis *could* bend, when they wanted to, I discerned. Good to know.

The appointment of a durable power of attorney for health care is a legal document that seemed to be misunderstood by many of the staffers at Borealis. I say this because Sam's daughter, Tammy, had no say in his health care if Sam was "decisional," and that he was, but of course, maybe not at two in most mornings, and that is where the gray came, I supposed, for them. I was not sure, however, if the decision of "no sedation" was Tammy's or Sam's, or most likely Tammy's as a back-up to Sam's. But to hear the staff talk, one would think the decision was totally Tammy's, and that thinking is just not correct, though common.

At this point, the question probably arises: how was I able to harvest the "goods" on Sam or the other residents in a health-care world that claimed stringent confidentiality? Well, during Sam's episodes, I always made sure I asked some staffer, "What is his name again?" My night-time forgetfulness/disorientation served to help the staff dismiss the interest of a woman who could not even recall the name of the man she played cards with every afternoon. It worked. They let me watch and listen without a thought of protecting his privacy from little ole forgetful me, who was the only resident surfacing at that late hour.

But, indeed, there would be a price to pay for this information when I would reckon with this ruse later, and later, in the wee hours of examining both the professional and personal sides of my guilt-ridden soul.

After weeks of watching Sam navigate through his night terrors—and bear in mind, Sam *could* have hurt someone—I felt like I was watching a scene from *Groundhog Day*: the time was always the same or close to the same, and with rare exceptions, all the players' lines and reactions were the same, including facial expressions. Being a nurse, I had the tendency to focus on the staff's handling of the situation. But once it came clear that I was seeing reruns, I decided I would try to block out the staff and focus on Sam.

It all started each night, between one and two in the morning, with Sam getting up in a sweat, leaving his room, and walking towards the community room which was openly connected to the dining room. He would go to the full-wall window and look out to the well-lit front grounds—oops, "campus." He would bang on the window, and then run towards the lobby. If no one tried to stop him, and it was rare that someone did, he would run for the front door. Visiting hours were of course over, so the door was always locked, and Sam would bang on the door. "Let me out!" he would shout. "God damn it, let me out. I have to go."

One staffer would insist he needed the toilet and would try to take him to the lobby restroom. Fortunately, she only worked part-time. Sam would resist her efforts to steer him towards the john, resist with everything he had at that late hour, which thankfully was not much. Eventually, he would always end up crying, and after he'd start crying, he would acquiesce, appearing to be physically and emotionally spent. He would walk back to his room, crawl into bed slowly, and pull the covers over his head. Across from his room, in my room, I could hear him whimpering like a pup searching for its mom. As he passed me in the hall, we almost always made eye contact, and it was hard to imagine that he might not recognize the woman with whom he spent every afternoon, humbling her at cards. And, in my defense, that was why I just had to bring up the subject that day.

During our afternoon games, Sam asked me questions about my life: family, job, home. I asked him questions back, but I must admit that I had become somewhat obsessed with trying to win at cribbage and this drive was throwing me off my real game of taking him in, as in doing my homework. I did learn that his wife died of cancer in their twenty-sixth year of marriage and that he never remarried. During our first game, I recalled that he had mentioned only that he had a daughter. But weeks later, when I asked how many children he and Jane had, he answered two, a boy and a girl. Gotta love that her name was Jane, unless, perhaps, you are a Nancy. I reasoned that likely his first answer had something to do with me talking about my daughter, or more likely, my memory had just failed me.

Sam told me proudly that he was an entomologist for the Wisconsin Department of Agriculture.

"Bugs, right?" I said.

"Yep, plant protection division."

"Wow. You must have to be smart to do that, Sam."

He answered quickly, like this was a well-worn line for him, "Well, I don't know about smart, but some say you have to be a pest to know a pest."

I was probably the only woman in Borealis who did not wear incontinence pads or briefs, but I could have used one after that line. And as I think back, his line was not really that funny; perhaps it was more that he was finally being funny with me that got me going. I needed humor, especially there. And I felt almost giddy having something to laugh about.

I told him I thought nurses and entomologists had a lot in common because we were both about getting to the bottom of things that were bugging the living. "Like for me, a nurse, it might be fungus under a pendulous breast, and for you?"

He laughed hard, a first for me to hear. He had a deep, smooth, melodious laugh. "Well, let's see, maybe people who don't understand insect cycles and bug the hell out of the department to 'get to work and handle those army worms that are eating all the leaves off our trees.' Like we can or should interfere with insect cycles."

He had said the quote in a female, crackly, curmudgeon-like voice, and, not expecting, I was spritzing again. I would have called Jeff on making the curmudgeon a woman, but I was in no mood to get out of our mood. I had so missed this type of banter since Jeff, whom I married largely because his dry sense of humor often made me laugh.

It came to mind at that moment that this had been the first time I had laughed at Borealis. It caused me to think back to the people I had met there, and I could not recall anyone laughing, except on a couple of occasions a burst of laughter spilling out of the staff office. Residents *smiled*—not a lot, but they smiled. And the staff smiled at the residents—mostly "I'm waiting" smiles, as in those smiles delivered while waiting for a resident who needs assistance with medication administration to methodically take each pill in order, their personally prescribed order, for personally defined reasons. But these were mostly puppet smiles, such that when the resident would look up at the waiting staffer, the staffer would do the quick up/down facial muscle flex and release, like someone just pulled a string from behind them, delivered to hide their mounting frustration.

But why weren't residents laughing? I wondered. Was nothing funny? Had we lost our sense of humor? Our sense *for* humor? Were we concerned about timing or appropriateness? Were we sad? Or was it that chronic pain had zapped what was left of our energy, leaving little or no oxygen to power our laughs or even find humor in the first place?

Gerontologists tell us that pain is not a normal change of aging, but I say give me the names of the seventy-plus-year-olds who have no pain and I'll show you their headstones. Or their prescription. It is true that the old will often deny pain, but I happen to be among the many who believe that this has to do with the old equating the word "pain" with acute pain, and that our denial reflects that equation. Not to mention the possible worry of what will be done to them if they admit to pain or the fact that they may worry that they no longer possess the organs necessary to detoxify and excrete the drugs that might relieve their pain. Dig deeper than a pain scale and the truth will be told. In my opinion, based on both my professional and personal experience, chronic pain is not only a change experienced during aging, but living with chronic pain is a developmental task of "later maturity" that Havighurst missed. And it is a big one, all too often thieving our energy, our love for life, our joy.

Assuming I had not spent enough time at Borealis to analyze the dearth of laughter, I decided to tuck away the question for further seasoning. But I can now admit that what I was really doing was suppressing, afraid of the answer, afraid my mounting aches and pains were the answer, and that my laughter had a death sentence.

* * *

It took a while before I had the nerve to bring this up to Sam, mainly because I thought it was getting too personal, but I felt I had to do it. "Sam, have you ever been told you look like Ronald Reagan?" He paused, and then dry-winked and wisecracked, "What took you so long, Ace?" He had started calling me "Ace" ever since the first time I beat him at cribbage, which occurred somewhere in the vicinity of a match that numbered well into double digits. And then, modulating his tone to a warmed-caramel smooth, he delivered, "Mr. Gorbachev, tear down this wall." It was near pitch perfect, and I would have bet it had once been perfect, a moist voice ago. After that performance, I started calling him "Dutch." And I hoped Nancy and Jane did not mind.

His wit, a sign of a good mind, was curious to me. In my professional experience, the ability to process and use beyond slap-stick-level humor effectively, not to mention being a master card player, was lost early in persons with cognitive changes. And if he was not physically disabled enough to warrant Borealis, what else but his mind could it be? The night-time episodes? He needed a shrink for that, not a nu-assisted living facility.

One game, I bluntly asked him, "Why are you here, Sam?"

He pulled his invisible school paper away from me and against his chest, and quipped, "Eyes on your own paper."

Oh God, will Sam ever forgive me?

He took a deep sigh and added sadly, "Another day, another game, Ace." I found myself focusing on why Sam was in that place and not in his own home, and this was seriously affecting my writing, not to mention my cribbage game. He could walk independently, only occasionally using a cane when his "lame went game." He once referred to "back trouble," offering only that he had injured his back a long time ago in an accident. He obviously could dress himself, because he was impeccably turned out, with stiff forward-point collared shirts underpinning somewhat form-fitting, mostly earth-tone, solid V-neck sweaters. No one that was staff-assisted for dressing looked that put together. His dockers and even his jeans looked pressed. My husband's clothes never looked that good, and I was starting to feel guilty about that, which was what eventually provoked me to delve: "Who does your clothes?" I felt better when he told me he sent them out—I am okay with not being able to compete with professionals, outside of my field. *He sent them out. From an assisted living facility.* Impressive.

Likewise, his Ken Cole cap toes were polished, and I mean highly polished, as in I could smell the Kiwi paste whenever I dropped a card and had to fish for it under the table. I happened to know a thing or two about menswear; Jeff's brother owned a menswear shop in the Cities, and we had occasion to babysit the business during their vacations.

And he smelled good. Now, I did have my Dolce & Gabbana Light Blue in my hand ready to pack for Borealis, but when I then thought back to my nursing home experiences, I recalled that, when those places weren't overpowered with the malodors of uncontained body fluids, they smelled like women's make-up and cheap cologne over what remained of those objectionable au naturel scents—the cosmetic squirt gals would probably call this "fragrance layering." The resultant stimulus to my olfactory receptors was what turned me off long ago to make-up foundation, and I did not want that to happen to my appeal for Dolce & Gabbana. But this place was not a nursing home and it smelled pretty good, most days; I should have brought it.

My assessment of Sam's reason for being at Borealis came up short; I still could not figure out why he was there. I gave up, wondering if we were working on the same book.

Sam and I soon became the Charles and Diana of Borealis. We were teased by staff about our relationship, and we fielded frequent whispered, walk-by commentaries such as, "Aren't they cute?" "Think there'll be a wedding?" Neither of us had a hearing problem. If I were staying at Borealis and I was really who I was pretending to be, I probably would have seen the need to set them straight, but then again if I was really who I was pretending to be, they might have been spot on.

The best-kept secret in that community room was that Sam and I were playing a high-level game of cribbage. Between Sam's "off" nights and my fake "off" days, I was quite sure the staff assumed we were playing no real game at all. They probably figured us to be on par with the twin sisters, Marge and Marian, who played cards with each other, each playing a different game, at the same time. Best I could figure, Marge was trying to play her version of euchre and Marian was attempting hearts, alternating their decks daily. Marge's deck had a joker in it, my first clue. When I asked why they rotated decks, Marge explained that she became suspicious when Marian's winning streak "grew longer than her nose" (they were identical twins), so she demanded they use her deck. Then apparently Marge's streak got no further than three when Marian balked, and they compromised to a daily rotation of their personal decks.

Neither appeared cognitively impaired during our dinner conversations, but their card-playing certainly made me wonder. I so wanted to ask them what game they were playing, but then I had the vision of ruining their fantasy journey when their responses would not match. The equivalent of an intentional Santa slip—I just could not do it. And if the staff caught full wind of the twins' game (games), would they be playing cards down the road? On second thought, maybe not, census was not full, and they were a twofer.

Or maybe the staff thought we were like Jasper who played air guitar with Buck Owens on "Hee Haw" and who, when I watched closely one Sunday evening, was darn close to the movement of both of Buck's hands.

And then there was Loretta, who knitted every waking, non-eating moment, with her fingers, twirling the yarn around and about her digits with no product save for a tangled ball of yarn. But if someone asked her, she knew she wasn't really knitting, and that was important for her to know because if she didn't, she'd also probably be evaluated for taking a road trip across that grey line between assisted living and the earthly final stop.

Loretta once owned a yarn shop called "Yarn Over," in one of the Twin Cities, and she lived in the other. She had spent a lifetime feeling yarn, and so it made perfect sense when she told me that she just liked the feel of yarn moving through her fingers. It calmed her, she said, as knitting had done for all her knitting life. Not long before I came to Borealis, she had been for real knitting with real needles, making knitted dolls that lined the shelves in her room and the rooms of other female residents. But then she had the misfortune of rolling over onto one of her knitting needles during the night, impaling her abdomen to enlarge her supplemental feeding tube stoma by two sizes, a feeding tube she had cared for by herself for decades, so it had made the Borealis cut. The impaling episode plus her declining eyesight were the reasons she gave up knitting.

Loretta took me to her room once to show me her knitted dolls. She said she started making the dolls when she first came to Borealis. When I inquired as to what led her to choose the making of dolls, she answered, serious as a heart attack, "When I got here, my daughter suggested I make friends." I moved on.

When I asked Loretta if she crocheted, leading to my eventual point that a crochet hook was more safely shorter and blunt compared to knitting needles, she replied that she had tried crocheting long ago but didn't like it because she liked making smaller projects. She wasn't an afghan or throw person, she said. She admitted, however, that it was much easier to recover from a mistake in crocheting than in knitting. "In knitting you have to thread all the loops back on your needle when you make a mistake, but in crocheting all you have to do is just pull your working thread back to the mistake. And a missed stitch doesn't unravel in crocheting like it does in knitting." She looked off to the window that was casting warm sun and bright light on her unprotected eyes and added, squinting, and tearing up, "Life should be like that, like crocheting."

I watched her fingers fake-knit for a considerable while after that comment, in large part because it was taking me that long to process her last thoughtful remark. As I watched, I noticed that every so often she would shake her head like something was wrong with her yarn work and then she would rearrange the yarn until an expression of satisfaction coupled with an affirmative nod conveyed that all was better. And I wondered who or what in her life she was pretending to do over, pretending to fix.

This was who they thought Sam and I were—the twin sisters, Jasper, Loretta. No one had a clue that Sam and I were really playing close to a tournament level of cribbage, well at least Sam was, or that Jasper could finger a guitar, or that Loretta was capable of deep thought. Or, most importantly, that even though the sisters were not playing the same game, they were enjoying the same game, and that was really all that mattered. That made me smile most days, wondering what, if any, other secrets were being stored in the eyes and ears of those Borealis walls, and if anyone knew that Loretta, much like Madame Defarge, was doing more than manipulating yarn in the tale of her two cities.

* * *

It seemed to me that the closer it got to Christmas, the longer were Sam's nightly episodes and the more intense were his displays of agitation. Or, I wondered, did his anguish just appear worse juxtaposed against an atmosphere of holiday decorations and continuous Christmas carols that bellowed from loudspeakers, pausing only for visiting community carolers and *Wheel*? More likely, I eventually concluded, it was that by then Sam was not the only one of us who was suffering.

One night, as I watched Sam leave his room in his panicked state, it occurred to me that he might be going to that window to see something. The next morning, up and about much earlier than usual, driven, I sat at a table near the window where Sam would always stand at the beginning of his episodes, and there I took in all that Sam could see from that viewpoint.

There was a half-circle drive-up with pillars on each side, but he would only be able to see half of it from where he would usually stand. A long entrance driveway was lined on both sides with birch trees. On the far side of that drive was a walkway and a couple of benches along the walk. He could see most of that. On the other side was a small pond with a short dock and a fountain in its center. He could see all of that. The fountain was, of course, turned off for the winter. And lights—a dozen or more antique-style streetlamps illuminated the driveway, plus white Christmas lights warming the naked arms of those birch trees.

The staff and residents, a mixture of Wisconsinites and Minnesotans in that border land, called the pond a lake, but trust me—I am from northern Minnesota—it was a pond. And that was it—no scary statues, no odd-shaped ornamental evergreens, nothing I could see that seemed in the least bit frightening. Nothing that would precipitate an emotional reaction. It was not anything he was seeing outside, I decided.

Vexingly, it was not only his nighttime behavior that was puzzling. Once when Andy visited, I introduced him to Sam as we passed in the hallway. Sam was so incredibly warm towards Andy that I was touched. He gave Andy a two-handed handshake and did not seem like he would ever let go. Andy's eyes met mine and uneasily said to me, "Is he okay?" and I smiled back a "Yes," but truthfully, I was not quite sure. When I looked at Sam during the handshake, I noticed that his forever dry eyes were welled with moisture. I had never seen his eyes wet before.

After the introductions, Sam followed Andy and me to the visitors' lounge. He stayed with us for Andy's entire visit. It was just fine with me, and God bless my son for acting like it was fine with him, too. I didn't know what to make of Sam following us—only days earlier, he had merely offered a "Pleased to meet you" to Bonnie, followed by a quick request to be excused to make a call. I wondered if the difference had anything to do with his energy level, thinking back to compare his nightly episodes before each of these two visits. But, as I looked back over my notes, I saw no obvious connection. Uncomfortable with young women? Perhaps just a guy thing? I would have to pay more attention to his interactions

When I could get the mystery of Sam out of my mind, writing came easy to me at Borealis, there where I was forced to face my own mortality during every contact I made with the hallways of the past, stored in the eyes of those who were counting their days and counting on their days left. I became adept at reading frustration, sadness, worry, anger, confusion, pain, and less often happiness, noticing the subtle changes in my fellow residents' behaviors that signaled change. I wondered why I could not do that consistently before. Perhaps because I had a life outside of my employ that distracted me from attending? Or was it that I began to see myself in these people, so close in time to being them, and I wanted to believe I would be noticed?

I became as charged as a new Duracell. Writing became effortless. Thoughts bounced around in my head as never before, like the balls in the air-blower bingo machine during Wednesday night bingo. I got really into Wednesday night bingo—I was way luckier than Sam.

Sam went home with his daughter for Christmas, and I went home with Andy, whose turn it was to have Christmas. When we returned, I wanted so badly to ask Sam if he had spells during any of the three nights he was away, but after the one and only time I had asked him whether he recalled his episodes, his cryptic reply had told me to never go there uninvited.

I had an okay Christmas. I really hated having to toss in some bizarre behavior to affirm my need to remain institutionalized, but duty called. I thought through my repertoire of antics from the list I had made. Some I had already used at Borealis—never in front of Sam, though—and some were family-specific, so those were mostly untried. All were inspired by my former patients and my then current co-residents, and each brought back a memory of the person to whom the behavior belonged, making it increasingly difficult to act out the role. I felt like I was betraying them—the type of guilt I had felt long ago after my sister and I would perform less-than-becoming take-offs on Mom and Dad. Our father would have called us smart alecks. Our mom would have just looked disappointed in us. But they never caught us, and I wish they would have—it went on too long.

My Christmas performances were successful, all of them. I poured gravy in my coffee cup and drank it without uttering a word. I told Bonnie she had a nice brother and that their parents should be very proud of them. I asked Andy if he knew my husband. After a few of these eye-rolling head-turners, I would slip back into me-land again—some would call it reality—and we had Christmas as usual. My Christmas gift to them was that I concentrated these performances within a short period of time so as not to ruin their whole Christmas, and I stayed clear of engaging the grandchildren in any of the above, except for the gravy, which those young hearts found delightfully humorous.

I know they will never completely forgive me, God, but I have settled on hoping for them to not disown me. Can you give me that, God, if You, Yourself, aren't too angry? disappointed? annoyed? with me? I so wish You would share Your feelings with me.

In late January, Sam had the worst-ever night terror. He threw a chair at the dining room window, cracking it. He scratched a nurse when he tried to push her away. My heart broke that night. His long Ronny face reminded me of the ancient Greek tragedy mask, Melpomene, the Muse of Tragedy—tormented, tortured, and the long hallway down which he made his spent return to his room, his Via Dolorosa.

He did not come to the dining room to eat or play cards the next day. I wondered if they were planning his transfer. I thought about visiting him in his room, but I had never done that before and it seemed that it would be intrusive to do so when he had made his need for privacy surrounding that matter crystal clear to me. I missed him. I missed me with him. I worried about him, and I worried about me without him.

Angie

That first afternoon without Sam turned into an awakening as to how Sam in my life at Borealis had diverted me from my mission. I found the community room to be wondrously filled with people I should have been meeting when I was playing cards with Sam. That realized, I still missed him. I kept looking towards the hallway that opened to our rooms, hoping I would spot his tall, gangly well-dressed figure ambling around the corner, looking for me. But deep down I knew better. His last night at Borealis had been bad, very bad.

My fear of Borealis requiring that Sam relocate began to rise in my soul like a cresting river post storm, especially when I heard one of the staff utter "sniff" in reference to Sam within a sentence that I could not quite hear in its entirety. Sniff is the phonetic pronunci-ation of the acronym SNF, as in skilled nursing facility—the three words Borealis residents never want to hear in reference to them-selves. The thought that he would be leaving Borealis (if I am being honest here, the thought that he would be leaving me) loomed like awaiting my first round of radiation and chemo. No, worse.

In a state of what I was hoping was only short-term loneliness, I decided to try to make a new friend, or at least a new acquaintance, probably more for my sanity than my project. Along the wall, in one of two grey faux leather wingback chairs, set up as a grouping for two, I spotted Angie. I had dinner with her once. We had chatted about the kolacky—both our mothers were Polish. Angie used a walker and oxygen, and she was blind.

There were several Borealis residents who were blind or near blind, mostly due to diabetes. As I saw it, their problem with losing their sight was not so much related to their actual visual deficits as the fact that these people had gone too long relying on sight, and that by the time they became blind, they were running low on the coping skills that would probably have facilitated their adaptation to this sensory loss, in some earlier time. That is, using a broad brush here, they had outlived the high-level ego defenses required to adjust to new-onset blindness or deafness or any other losses, for that matter. And of course, some, as would be true of any subpopulation, never carried a full suitcase of those skills from their get-go. Not to mention that in cases of mild cognitive impairment, as in fake-me, their old coping skills often leave at higher rates than they do in plain old aging, used up in dealing with the stress of recognizing their developing cognitive impairment—the I'm-not-who-I-was stressor.

I got to thinking: maybe I should spend one day a week *not* relying so much on my eyesight, and one day *not* relying so much on my hearing, and one day *not* relying so much on my memory—that would be tough, because how do you not remember to not remember? —and one day not relying so much on walking. And on and on. But on Sundays, I would get to be the whole package. I figured I would be tuning up those adaptation skills that I would someday need to adjust to eventual deficits. That afternoon, I was not relying so much on Sam, and *oh dear God, I wished it were Sunday.*

Angie clutched her purse, or "handbag," as the seriously old called them, like every woman did at Borealis. In fact, the first and only other time I had encountered Angie was the day I decided to start carrying a purse, having realized I was the only woman of the four at the dinner table who didn't have one on my lap. This purse fixation, I surmised, was perhaps in part because of the habit these women had of having their purses with them whenever they left their homes, BB (before Borealis), which meant to me that residents, at least female residents, considered their home to be their room and not the whole of Borealis. And another part of this for some was the underlying mistrust of staff and other residents, which few spoke about verbally, but which was communicated loudly and clearly with a variety of nonverbal cues, purse-clutching being just one.

I had never been in the habit of carrying a purse; I like pockets. Bibs have a lot of pockets. So, taking my purse along, at first, was a difficult piece to remember, yet soon after I started, I was surprised to find that I was starting to become uncomfortable leaving my room without it. However, whereas *taking* my purse along became a habit, *clutching* it like a lifeline had yet to come for me—I tended to leave it here and there, mostly there. All that was in my small suede cross-body bag was a mini package of nose wipers, a deck of cards, and "our" travel cribbage board.

"Hi Angie. Can I join you for a visit?" She looked up in my direction but cocked her head like she hadn't a clue. "Joni Bohne, remember? My mother had a freezer dedicated to her frozen kolacky?"

Angie smiled, probably more to the kolacky reference than my name I assumed (although many smile to the rhyme and the irony inherent in the fact that I am not thin), and then she reached for the other chair, struggling to stretch and tap it. I was slightly taken aback by this gesture. It would have been so much easier for her to just say, "Sure, have a seat."

Angie wore dark glasses. A maroon and olive bohemian canvas drawstring bucket bag lay on her lap along with several pieces of balled-up facial tissue, her lap a substantial piece of real estate to accommodate this assemblage. She was a "drooler," her speech having been affected by a stroke, but not badly. I could understand every word she said, although my past included a career of listening to phone orders from sleepy doctors, many with heavy accents.

At first, not being able to see Angie's eyes made the task of interpreting her nonverbal communications more difficult for me, causing me to realize that I tended to rely heavily on eye contact. But I soon recognized that the rest of her face made-up for this deficit. Two horizontal cheek dimples opened and closed to display her level of joy like music spectrum visualizers, while prominent zygomatic arches raised and lowered like drawbridges, allowing entry to her smile. Angie's face was a warm face—smooth, supple, creamy—it said she wanted to talk with me. Her face *did* get some additional help from her silky silvery curls, though, framing her face like piped frosting on a birthday cake.

Even with all this warmth being communicated, I struggled with what to say next. Odd, if she were my patient, I would not have hesitated about how to start our conversation but courting a friend when I was lying about who I happened to be was another story, and I felt at a loss for words.

"Angie, so, tell me about yourself?"

She chuckled. "I haven't been asked that for as long as I can remember." She paused and wiped the drool from her mouth. "What do you want to know?"

All I really wanted to know at that moment was how Sam was doing, but I shook off that feeling as best as I could and answered, "Whatever you want me to know." I started to worry that I was sounding too therapeutic, but then I relaxed with the thought that I had never lied about having been a nurse, so I should still have some of these skills. I raised my brows and smiled a sassy smile that she could not see and said, "Tell me something . . . interesting."

Another wipe of her mouth, and then she said, "I was a nun once. How 'bout that for interesting?"

I paused for a retake on this woman, trying to picture her in a long habit, veil, hands tucked under her scapular, glide-walking in fast baby steps over a highly waxed tiled floor, but I couldn't quite see it.

"Wow. Talk about interesting. Now, are you serious Angie, or are you playing with me here?"

"Damn serious."

Now that was funny. I bellowed out a cackle that made the laugh-deprived walls of Borealis take notice. I forgot what I had learned in nursing school about communicating with the blind when I touched Angie's knee without warning her, but she didn't seem startled by my misstep, and then I said, "You have to tell me the whole story, Angie, from the beginning."

She scooped her damp balled-up facial tissues from her lap, accidentally forwarding one to the floor, stuffed them into a side pocket of her bag, and then reached into her bag for a new supply. She arranged these carefully across her lap. I took this as a sign that she had a lot to tell me.

"I was in the Dominican order," she paused for breath, and then added, "for the square root of forty-nine years." I quickly did the math and concluded that the seven-year itch was a problem for people no matter whom they married. But why did she say it that way? During her pause, I could feel her eyes searching my face, if only they worked.

She continued, "I left the convent for a tailor. He was an apprentice to the man who made our habits . . . and I became *the* example of why men . . . should never be allowed inside convent walls." She laughed! It was a rare-to-be heard-in-Borealis hearty, belly laugh, causing mega drool and a gasp for additional oxygen. After she replenished the breath her laugh had stolen, she continued: "We could never have children. Abe was convinced that the convent . . . had put something in our food or drink to make us sterile." Angie's raised left eyebrow, which peeked above her glasses, combined with her smashed sandwich smile, suggested to me that she might be convinced of this conspiracy as well, but that she did not trust me enough to say so aloud. Her smooth and quick, obviously well-practiced, eyebrow move made me think that she probably was not blind her entire life, perhaps a complication of diabetes.

In the course of a half hour, Angie did not pause except to wipe her mouth or wait for breath. Her nasal cannula was only cannulating one nostril ever since she had snagged it during a mouth-to-cheek wipe early in her discourse. It took every ounce of professional restraint I could summon to not adjust that cannula. I rationalized that it was not slowing her down, because her syllable-to-breath ratio was stable throughout her tale, at or around ten, and her lips were still as pink as they were when she started, which was more in hue with mauve.

She explained that she had earned her degree in education with a math emphasis, while in the convent, and had barely worked off her tuition at the Catholic school that shared a furnace with the convent when the "lovebug bit."

"We were married two score plus days that numbered . . . the angle degree of an isosceles . . . when he slumped at the wheel of his Chevy truck in his twenty-first prime year . . . which is supposed to be the best number . . . because seventy-three is the twenty-first prime . . . and its mirror, thirty-seven, is the twelfth prime . . . and its mirror, twenty-one, is the product of . . . seven and three, back to seventy-three. Get it? . . . But it was not the best year for us."

I wanted to ask her to repeat the math riddle but thought better of sucking her dry of oxygen. So, while she rearranged her lap dresser, I repeated the phrase "seventy-three twenty-first prime mirror" five times in my head so I could figure it out later. And later I did, and I was enchanted.

She seemed so with it, so normal, except for this math thing going on. I had to ask, "You speak in math problems, Angie?"

"Yes. I do. Does it bother you?" She looked up towards my face, like she was reading my nonverbal cues, except about thirty degrees off. "It bothers some."

"I wouldn't say it bothers me," *yet*, I thought, and added, "Intrigues me, for sure."

"That means you want to know why, right?" she teased, brandishing an intent-to-disclose smile.

"Right." I smiled another wasted smile and wondered, like that falling forest tree, if a smile falls on a face and no one is there to see it, does it send a message?

Her adjusted smile said to me that it did, that probably my smile was one with my tone.

Grabbing even shorter breaths between phrases, she started to explain: "Well, in the convent, I had a roommate . . . who was a French teacher for far longer . . . than I had been teaching math. She said the key to teaching a foreign language . . . was to never speak in anything to your students . . . but the foreign language. I got to thinking about math and how it was like . . . a foreign language to my students . . . and then I decided never to say . . . out loud any number, outright, directly . . . and I used math problems instead. At first it was hard, but I got really good at it . . . and my students got really good at math as a result."

I was good at math. I liked playing this game. But I had to fix that cannula. Her rescue breaths were getting longer and more frequent. At least this time I remembered to ask if I could touch her before I did, and as I adjusted the clear green tubing, I asked, "Did you talk like that all the time, even with Abe—that was his name, right, Abe?"

"Yes, Abe. No, I only talked like that in the classroom." At the mention of his name, she removed her glasses and searched for a fresh tissue. And then she wiped her eyes. "Even after all these years, he still gets me going." The end of that statement came out as a sob. And then a deep breath, the size of which I didn't think she had left in her, gave way to, "So, why do I talk this way here, I bet you want to know."

"Yes," I replied, still wasting nods. "I've been wondering."

"I guess I started doing it here . . . to make me stand out. Around here if you don't stand out . . . you are absorbed into these walls . . . Maybe it keeps my mind a bit sharper, who knows . . . Maybe it takes me back to a time when I felt most like me." She felt for the wall behind her and missed. "I swear, sometimes when I sit here . . . I feel like I can hear the people that were here before us . . . begging to be released from these walls."

I wish I had not felt the need to change the subject, but I did, and I did so by asking, "Abe, was he . . ."

"Jewish? Yes. Isn't that a story in itself? A nun marrying a Jew. When I broke out, I really broke out!"

"You changed religions?" I said, embarrassed by my unintended squeak.

"Oh no." She smiled a broad smile and sucked in a pint-sized breath before she continued, "We looked at it this way: I saw it that Abe did not recognize Christ . . . as the Son of God, and he saw it that I was jumping the gun . . . recognizing a great and wonderful teacher . . . as the Son of God. We were both Christians of a sort . . . We both loved Christ's message . . . We both ordered our footsteps on His Word. But I would have upper-cased the His . . . and he would have lower-cased it. That's all the difference we figured we had to live with . . . and we lived with it just fine. I always teased him that I knew a savior when I saw one. He teased back with 'Who you talkin' about, me?'" She released that belly-jiggling laugh again, followed by a multi-tissue mouth-wipe and several tissues finding the floor.

She grabbed for a new tissue, and wept, "But he was so right; he *was* my earthly savior."

And then I got a chance to feel that smooth, supple, creamy cheek of hers, against mine.

We spent almost two hours in each other's company, Angie answering the many unanswered questions I had about many of the residents and staff. She tried hard to engage me about my life story, but my steering wheel was not powered for that discussion. I boomeranged those questions back to her mainly because the telling would eventually cause me to lie to this very true and real woman. She saw through that and said, "You don't like talking about yourself, do you?"

Angie did not need eyes.

At four, when her smart watch alarm sounded, she announced, "It's the square root of sixteen. Time to get ready for dinner." Then she smiled, and I thought I saw her right cheekbone rise and expose the evidence of a wink behind the dark glasses. "Actually, what I really have to do, dear lady, is take a little shot that allows me to have two of those kolackies. But first will you help me point my garbage stabber on those tissues that I'm sure I have dropped? Just stab the stick in each one for me and I'll do the rest."

Tammy and Sam

That evening, around the *square root of one hundred minus three* o'clock, I spotted Sam's daughter, Tammy, short for Tamarack, walking like a mother about to break up a serious fight between her children—fast and furious, in stilettos.

I had met Sam's daughter once when she had visited him. She was easy to spot—hair cut to one inch and spiked, with the one and only shape of face and type of hair that could successfully pull that off. Her scant hair sparkled, probably from whatever product made it stiff, and her eyes followed suit. She had one of those waists that women with my kind of waist cannot take their eyes off for wondering what it would be like for just one day . . .

And when it came to her sense for apparel, like father, like daughter. I never knew anyone who looked good in eggplant, much less stunning as did Tammy in a suit with too many darts to count. Even Leonard, who came in second behind Bert for fewest words, hundred-something Leonard, uttered a no-doubt-about-it "wow" when she passed him. He was near blind, so maybe it was her amazing fragrance.

Few people fooled me when it came to their age thanks to a game that I played during my forty-plus-year nursing career. I had always made quick rounds on my patients before I received report from the off-going nurse so that I could picture the person when I was receiving information about them during verbal report. And so, during those pre-conference rounds, without looking at my census, I would silently guess their age and their weight, within thirty seconds of our meeting. I scored a point if my guess was within plus or minus one year and another point if within ten pounds. I had a 97 percent average by the time I retired—yes, I kept track on my hardboard clipboard, ones and zeros, a *bit* ahead of my time?

But Tammy was a challenge. From a distance, it was hard to believe she could be any Borealis resident's child. She appeared to be in her early to mid-thirties, but I knew she could not be that young. Sam had mentioned that he and Jane married late, waiting for Jane to finish her master's degree in education, but the way Tammy looked and moved, and doing the math with what little I knew, *that* late would likely have been too early for Jane to have conceived this young-appearing woman.

From her stride, I figured she knew about what happened with Sam the night before. As she got closer and no slower, I doubted whether she would even remember me, but she did. She came to a quick stop about three feet from me and shot, "Joni, how was he last night?" Like she had *expected* bad, but did not know? Like she expected *me* to know? Had Sam talked about me to her? I felt a pang of guilt shoot through my sclerosing veins when I realized I had put that thought ahead of my concern for Sam. But that guilt was welcome—meant I was still *aware*.

"Tammy, he threw a chair. He shoved a nurse." My voice cracked like ice in warm soda. From three feet, I could see she was not in her thirties—definitely, at least, mid-forties. And why I was playing my age game at a time like that probably, I later thought, had much to do with that self-indulgent part of my personality that was responsible for me being at Borealis in the first place. More guilt…to appreciate.

Tammy broke me from my inapt calculations, "Oh my God, I had a feeling this wasn't going to be good. And then I woke up to a phone message that said he was okay but that he had a bad night and to come or call today."

Intrigued, because I seriously thought she was referring to some psychic leading, I reflected, "Had a feeling?"

"Yesterday was the anniversary of the accident. I knew I should have had him stay with us." She searched my face for understanding. Finding none, she continued, "He never told you about the accident, the accident that killed my brother?"

I sensed she was heading into territory that Sam would have explored with me, by then, if he had wanted me to know. If I let her continue, which she was clearly ready to do, I felt I would be invading Sam's privacy, and in doing so, I would be disloyal to Sam.

I took a deep breath for all the oxygen it would take to summon the nicest, gentlest nonverbal signals I was capable of to accompany this statement: "Tammy, I know only that you had a brother, Birch. Your father and I have spent dozens of hours together, one on one. If he wanted me to know more about this, he would have told me. So, out of respect for your father's privacy, I will end this conversation with, go to him, Tammy, and please let me know if there is anything I can do."

She scanned me up and down, trying, I imagined, to figure out the relationship between me and her father. I wanted so badly to say, "If you figure it out, clue me in, please."

I was never more frustrated in my entire often-frustrated life than when she walked away and I realized that I was so close, so darn close, to fitting another piece into my Sam puzzle, and damn if I hadn't choked. I had put Sam's feelings before my project, which did not sound awful until I considered that I had put my project before my children's feelings.

What in the hell is going on with me, God? I probably should not say "hell" to You, but I am forlorn.

* * *

Shortly after Tammy's visit, there was a knock on my door. I was deep in thought, journaling, so the knock startled me. Before I could think of what to do next, I heard, "It's me, Sam."

Sam? I hopped out of bed and opened the door a crack, not wanting him to see me in my long underwear. "Sam, hi, what's up? How are you?"

"Can you meet me in the community room? I need to talk with you." It had only been just over a day since I last saw him, but he looked pale and drawn and like he had lost weight.

"Sure. I'll be right there." I changed my clothes and threw on some mascara, having been cursed with peach fuzz for eyelashes.

Oh, please God, let it not be that he is leaving Borealis.

I met Sam in the community room and noticed he had uncharacteristically, and perhaps strategically, positioned himself so that he was facing away from the windows, most likely avoiding view of the boarded-up window that had so recently fielded the chair he tossed. I soon learned Sam *was* leaving Borealis, but not for good, at least he said he did not think so. He was going to Tammy's, leaving right after our talk, to be closer to the neurologist who was treating his "fright nights." He thought he would be gone for a week or two, spending his next-week birthday there for sure.

His mood reminded me of a flower that was weighted down with morning dew, unaware, poor thing, that sun and breeze would likely make it all better soon. He had very little else to say, and I didn't smile, as he slightly did, when he referred to his episodes as fright nights. I refrained from asking any questions because I was feeling slighted that he did not confide in me about his son's death, causing me to again sense that I had no right to information that he was not offering. *At least he searched me out to inform me about his plans before he left*, I comforted myself.

And as I thought about feeling hurt about Sam's lack of forth-comingness alongside my clandestine reason for being at Borealis, my "black kettle" left the room, but only after he gave me a hug that left enough space between the two us for another resident, and maybe even their walker, to slip between. *Happy Birthday, my dear Sam*, I said to the empty community room as I watched him drag his heartrending face in the direction his feet were escorting it.

Jeff and God

That night, after my brief encounter of the coolest kind with Sam, I talked to Jeff for a long, long time. I had been saying good-night to Jeff every night, ever since he died, adding all my other dead loved ones a few months into the practice when it just seemed the right thing to do. The list was mounting, by then up to some twenty friends and relatives who I imagined were standing or hovering or flying right next to my Jeff.

But that night I poured out my soul to Jeff in long voice and never got to those peripheral spirits. I told God that I was talking to Him, too, but that when it came to this subject, I could relate better to Jeff, and that He shouldn't be put out.

Jeff (and God) I have a special feeling for Sam, but I don't know exactly what that feeling is. It feels like a sincere liking, a type of affection, but it is so mixed with the fascination of wondering who he really is that I can't honestly say whether, if the mystery was not there or was solved, I'd still hold onto this feeling of affection, separate and distinct. Or is Sam just what makes this place bearable for me, which means I may have made a big mistake by coming here. And Jeff, I don't feel at all for Sam what I felt and still feel for you, but I don't have experience to know if any second love can be as good as a first good love. I said love, Jeff. Oh God, I said love. I hate that word since you aren't here. I don't think I know what it means or maybe I never knew what it meant, and our relationship gave me no reason to define it. Oh, that sounds awful, Jeff. I didn't mean it that way. Our relationship was comfortable, and I was content and never had reason to . . . Crap. Rewind—let me try this again. You and I grew up together, Jeff, not as kids, but as very young adults. And then we raised kids together. It wasn't all perfect, not even close, probably more my fault than yours that it wasn't, but there is no one word to describe all that joy, pain, passion, tenure. Sam and I have cards and conversation and mutual appreciation in a place where all of that is in very short supply. How could any one word have the nerve to assume it could capture both relationships? See what I mean, Jeff? I don't even like talking about love when it comes to Bonnie and Andy because the definition of love I held onto for so long as a mother would not have included driving a tractor over their feelings to write a book. But, Jeff, it's not about a book . . . It's about the purpose this book will serve. You believe that, don't you, Jeff? I believe that, don't I? I bet you know the answer to that question even when I am not sure I do. I'm scared, Jeff. I'm scared about what I've done. I'm scared of what I'll become: old and alone and spending the rest of my life with people who don't know or love me. Because probably no one will care about me after I did this to them, and I can't say that I'd blame them. And I'm afraid of spending another night talking to you when you never flipping answer me back! (I so wanted to use the real "f "word, for emphasis, but considering I was talking to God, too, well, I have my standards). *I'm sorry, Jeff, I don't hate you, but I hate that I'm the one left. You would have been a much better only parent left. I never asked you this Jeff, probably because I was afraid of the answer, but if you had a do-over shot, would you spend your life on me? I don't worry about having to answer that question any more than you do because YOU NEVER TALK TO ME! But really, looking back, isn't it crazy that these decisions about life partners are so often made when we are so very young and know nothing about most everything? But then look at me now, older, supposedly wiser, and I still don't know what I feel about just about everything. I used to play this game of looking at other men and wondering if I could spend my life with that man, or that one. Jeff, I never answered yes. And I'm not talking sex here, because I probably would have answered yes to a good third of them if that was what I was thinking about. I mean, come on, that's why I never played THAT game. The point is that, now when I look at Sam, I don't even play the could-I-spend-the-rest-of-my-short-life-with-him game because our lives together will end in so many months. If I pretend that we are BB, I still have no answer. I guess I am not comfortable with him like I was with you. Maybe I'm just comforted by him. I miss you, Jeff. And I miss Sam. But I miss him in the community room, and I miss you everywhere. You can't really hate me from heaven, can you, Jeff? I mean isn't heaven like a hate-free zone? God? Jeff? Are either of you listening? Do either of you care about how scared and lonely I am? Do I have to die to find out?*

And I didn't fall asleep talking to Jeff and God until I admitted to myself that who I was really talking to was *me*.

Goodnight God. Goodnight Jeff. Goodnight Joni.

No Sam

With Sam away, I continued to explore the community room scene. Though Sam and I played cards in that room most days, we didn't really pay much attention to what was going on, except for the occasional outburst of a television request or commentary. No exaggeration—some residents talked more to the television than to each other.

They—I guess I should say we—came close to becoming a family at Borealis, and much like in all families, there were different strokes that floated our different boats. There were conflicts and compromises. Most squabbles centered on what to watch on television, the volume of the television, and how much to open/close the blinds to better see the television. No wonder there were few homes for old folks before television, I decided. What would they have done with us?

On this day, a group of about a dozen were watching a news clip about an ice storm that was scaling the East Coast. Weather was of big interest at Borealis, which intrigued me because we were rarely in the weather, certainly not in any inclement weather. Furthermore, many residents claimed that, BB, the weather channel was their go-to station at home when nothing else interested them. Some claimed they left it on all day. Fascinating. Perhaps it was confirmation of their good fortune at no longer having to deal with inclement weather—a benny of aging?

Likewise, I mused, this was probably the reason why BB I had taken to watching cable news during much more of my day than I cared to admit, ever since retirement. Was the bad news comforting in that it exposed a world I would not so much mind leaving in my near future? Or was it just that the overwhelming hundred-plus stations had little to offer the likes of my generation? Earnestly (that is my new word for the overused "seriously"), "Cash Cab" and "My 600 Pound Life"?

The weather report that day was followed by a report on a missing teen. The teen was described as a "star of his high school football team and a straight-A student." Sebastian commented: "Would they not look as hard for him if he were a straight-D student?"

Angie and I were the only ones who laughed. Well, neither of us actually laughed, but rather we sort of chortled, reacting, of course, not to the story, but rather to Sebastian's take on the report. Angie put her hand to her mouth in a weak display of trying to catch her reaction, and I looked around to see if anyone noticed us because it really wasn't appropriate to make light of a story about a missing teen.

I thought we were home free and that either no one heard Sebastian, they did not process his sarcasm, or they did not hear us chortle. Yet, before I expelled the sigh of relief that was hanging in the hallway of my lungs, Arnie piped up with, "What's so funny?" Now, I was not sure if Arnie was chastising us for ill-appropriated humor or if he just wanted to get in on the joke. Angie and I kept silent and before we had a chance to formulate a reply, we were saved by the three bells of the community room clock.

"*Wheel of Fortune!*" was called out by more than half the TV watchers. Arnie shouted out, "*Decades!*" Bert quietly and defeatedly put in her daily bid for *Little House on the Prairie*. Several requests for *Golden Girls* precipitated groans from the men. The chatter went on for nearly a full commercial segment, but then was halted by the piercing voice of a resident who was referred to by many as the "Bingo Bitch." "*Wheel* has it!" she yelled, minus only a gavel . . . and a broom.

The Bingo Bitch's name was Sylvia. As I type this, it occurs to me that none of us knew each other's last names. In fact, it was during Sam's chair-throwing episode when I first heard his last name, overhearing a call to his doctor. Everyone—staff and residents—were on an exclusive first name basis, with one exception, me. I always introduced myself with my full name, and to residents I added that I was a resident. Even the staff's nametags displayed only their first names, when they were not flipped. So much of our identity was lost, I thought. Or was it?

The Bingo Bitch label was birthed in response to Sylvia's habit of insisting that the bingo caller ignore the requests of sluggish-thinking residents to slow down the call. "Don't play if you can't keep up" was the comment that earned her this brand.

Sylvia's eyebrows, which collectively resembled my best attempt at drawing birds in flight, were penciled in, thick, and nearly connected over her nose which pointed north. Platinum cotton candy hair was kept off the sides of her face with bobby pins, sometimes clips. Her five-shades-too-dark make-up ended abruptly an inch from her hairline, like she was wearing a mask—we could only hope. Her jewelry, albeit appearing tawdry, would make Cleopatra appear dull and unadorned. Add it all up, and she had a personality to match. I did not like this woman.

No one could figure out why Sylvia resided at Borealis. Her limbs and mouth were fluidly mobile; her brain was sharp, razor sharp. Arnie said she was there because no one in her family could stand her and she needed vulnerable people to bully. Arnie, however, did not use the word "vulnerable;" he used "suckers."

Alas, we were like a pack of canines: we had our alpha and our omega, and all the hierarchy in-between. The hounds just above the omega cozied up to alpha Sylvia for protection. Those just under avoided her, tolerated her, and once in a while raised their hackles at her. Again, the staff seemed unaware—maybe it was more of being uninvolved. As I watched her, I wondered if she ever cried. I just could not picture that.

Tom happened to be the keeper of the remote that day; it was an informal, rotating role from what I had been able to grasp. One had to miss dessert to grab that puppy. Before he was able to switch the channel, Arnie exclaimed, "We always watch *Wheel*. Bert never gets to see her show." With that, he broke the Borealis cardinal rule and hastily pulled himself upright using his walker instead of pushing off on the arms of his chair, and, surviving that unsafe behavior, he made his way over to Tom, extending his hand for the remote. Tom turned it over, smirking and winking, proud of Arnie for standing up to the Bingo Bitch.

Arnie was lean (well, by this time, most of the men left were lean) and a flashy dresser, stepping right out of the seventies in his mix-and-match leisure suits and coordinating long-pointed collar shirts, all of it 100 percent polyester and each piece sadly telling the tale of his Parkinsonian tremors that caused him to not be able to hold onto a cup of coffee without spillage. He smelled like a diner after hours if you got close enough. And how, with his shakiness, he had managed to trim and wax his handlebar stache was a frequent pondering among the ladies.

He was a romantic of sorts, stealing cookies from the ladies' trays, asking them to "scooch their keisters" if he wanted in at their table, spraying compliments like pollen on a breezy day—picaresque. Yet there was this: For Arnie, honesty was not an all or none—it was a sum (and that is not a typo.) He calculated the benefits and risks of that virtue like actuaries calculate insurance risks and premiums, and so he was the kind of guy, BB, who would bring "his woman" a spray of fresh flowers, yet no one would have been surprised to find out that he filched them off a roadside memorial. His calculation would likely be that it would not make the dead person who died there happy, as it would "his woman." The men saw through him, but they held back. His aura apparently demanded a level of respect.

But Arnie had a heart for the underdog, and Bert was all of that, so that day, as the *Little House* theme song blared in the community room, several wheelchairs and walkers could be heard squeaking and dragging away in retreat. Bert moved closer to the television, and as I caught a glimpse of a satisfied Arnie, I decided that he probably *had* been chastising Angie and me for our earlier chortle because down deep he was a champion of social justice.

Arnie retreated, not to his previous seat, but to a chair against the wall, a point from where he could take in the whole room. He leaned forward, elbows on the arms of the chair, *his* arms folded across his lap, and he did not watch *Little House*, but rather scanned the room lest any dissenters should surface. And something told me we would be watching *Decades* the following day.

Little House happened to be one of my favorite shows, also, so I stayed. And there it was! Crystal clear. Life imitating art. Bert's inspiration. The episode was about a woman who is certain that only her funeral will bring her distant family together, and so she convinces Doc Baker and the Ingalls to fake her death while she plans to happily celebrate her eightieth birthday, with her children . . . at her own wake.

I was familiar with the episode, so I pulled up a chair next to Bert and watched the rest of the episode alongside her. She never spoke or changed her somber expression, her eyes glued to the screen. Alongside her, I remained silent, also. She looked up at me once, and her eyes said she knew I knew. We sat there even after the episode was over, and still without words between us, we waited for dinner. When it was time, we moved to a table together, and we ate slowly, quietly, and meditatively like a couple of cloistered nuns, attempting to tune out the clinking and the chatter that began to sound to me like a bad case of tinnitus, both of us—I just knew—wishing it would have worked for her like it had on *Little House*.

* * *

In my short time at Borealis, I had gained seven pounds. The food was good, and I had been quite sedentary, by design. I could feel my clothes getting tighter, so I stepped on the scale that was sardonically located directly behind the dessert table in the dining area of the community room. The nerve.

My weight has always been a thorn. I started logging my weight in college where I brought my seven-year-old Petunia Pig (significant other of Porky Pig) spiral binder to accompany the bathroom scale (mechanical dial scale) that I received for opening my first checking account in our neighborhood bank, just before heading off to WIU. My plan was to ward off the "freshman twenty" that loomed above my fear of flunking out, for I possessed skills for the latter.

My skinny aunt had given me the pig notebook for my twelfth birthday, slipped in among a bunch of benign school supplies. She was the only skinny member of our extended family, and she had a way of making her skinniness known. Skinny belts, tucked-in pleated blouses, tucked-in comments—she messaged loudly and clearly. My mother, her sister, tried hard to convince me that there was no message in the pig notebook. I begged to differ. A smart pubescent, I knew my belly stuck out further than my breasts and that it should have been the other way around. I tossed that binder on the top shelf of my closet, and it stayed there until I was packing for college. But I always knew it was there. Every time I looked at that shelf, I thought about her message. And when I had finally scaled down for graduation and college and was worried about scaling back up in my first semester of limitless cafeteria food, I plucked it off the shelf and tucked it amidst my packed undies. It had power, that ole binder. It unstruck my craving chord, with just a glance. Exercising the will to look at it, however, was where its power ended.

During college, I stored the binder under the scale, and later, upon returning home, it hung from the balance scale that my mother inherited from Dr. Chott for whom she worked, after he upgraded to a digital scale. When I married and moved away from home, I went back to my old bathroom scale, until I later inherited the doctor's scale when weighing became too much for my mother (who couldn't stand unsupported), and unnecessary for my father, who was dead. I liked the old bathroom scale better than the doctor's scale, though, because I could get it to work for me if I tilted to the left.

Throughout the years, I recorded my weight in code—it kills me to reveal the code after so many years of it being a secret, but it was "REPUBLICAX." I stole this gem from the pharmacist I worked for when I was in high school. In his neighborhood "drug store" that smelled like vitamins and rubbing alcohol, and where I was his first female "soda jerk," no hat though, one of my jobs was to use this code to mark the cost of the pharmaceutical stock from McKesson and Robbins. Then, when dispensing, he knew how much to mark up from that number. He was a staunch Republican. I never got the "X" though.

There were just over fifty years of weight entries in that Petunia Pig notebook. It even went with me on vacations, sometimes even if I did not take the scale. Go *figure.*

Across the decades, I had gone through periods of weighing myself daily, weekly, and monthly. If I weighed weekly, it was always Friday, so I could eat on the weekend. If monthly, it was the first Friday of the month, same logic—perhaps you can see where this was heading. There were only two extended gaps of no entries: One was for two months before finals when I was nearly flunking organic chemistry and I needed comfort food in a big *weigh.* The other was for the four months after Jeff died—same justification.

I did not bring either of my scales with me to Borealis. I was hoping Borealis had one that was more compassionate. After I weighed myself at Borealis, I returned to my room and entered my weight in the barely-hanging-together Petunia Pig binder. Then, I flipped fast through the pages like a zoetrope, envisioning the images of my body in various shapes and sizes, across time. At one point, I paused when I came upon an entry I just could not believe—even major left scale tilting could not have accounted for that number. And that number persisted for nearly two months of daily entries before it slowly grew. It was a stunning minuend until I took my Borealis subtrahend and used it to calculate the difference, which turned out to be positive forty-eight. Squinting to make out the dates associated with the nadir of my decades' worth of weight recordings, I discovered that those all-time lows were recorded in the two months preceding our wedding. And then and there, in Borealis room 117, as I pulled my night shirt free of the two abdominal rolls that were clamping onto it like a clam in its prime, I decided to do what I had never before dared to do: add up the total pounds lost and gained in my half-century of archiving my fat.

The result was thus: in 52 years, 987 lost and 1,020 gained. Astounding.

My memory was jogged into reminiscing, and all the diets, wardrobe revamps, exercise programs, and orthopedic injuries came flooding into my thoughts like I was Albert Brooks on trial in *Defending your Life*. Low calorie, low fat, high protein, hi fat-low carb, eating with chopsticks (slowed me down), water, water, water, green tea, apple cider vinegar, weighing food, weighing me, step aerobics, shin splints, trampoline-frayed menisci, rowing rotator cuff tears, and my personal favorite—walking fast for twenty minutes, *exactly* twenty minutes after finishing every meal. Not nineteen, the book said, not twenty-one, but starting at exactly twenty minutes after taking my last bite of my meal. Actually, this twenty-minute gig was what I did before our wedding, and it worked. But my guess is that anything would have worked with the motivation of mega heirloom wedding photographs dancing in my foreconscious.

So, there I was, in Room 117, consoling myself with how big I might have become if I did not yoyo. And then I ate a Mars bar . . .

And I got to thinking about Mars—Inc., not the planet. Mars was the only candy bar I ever ate. Well, I did *try* them all, but Mars became my go-to, eventually going steady with it when I became pregnant with Andy. When I heard the news that the Mars bar would be discontinued, in 2000, I cried, and then I stocked up. I bought ten cases, froze them, and kept replenishing my supply whenever Mars, Inc would have short runs of revival on the chocolate-malt nougat bar covered with a mid-layer of caramel and a final layer of milk chocolate. Rumor had it that the same recipe was relaunched as the Snickers Almond Bar—do not believe everything you read—I could tell the difference. What has perplexed me, however, was that Mars Inc reported $33 billion in sales in 2015, yet they could not afford to keep a run of their namesake candy bar going. That is just not, well, you know, *right*.

Finally, after I did the math on my net gain, I found that if I subtracted that number from my current weight, I would be smack dab in the middle of my healthy BMI range—mind-blowing. I began to daydream about auctioning off my Petunia Pig notebook to Jenny Craig and Nutrisystem and Weight Watchers, the highest bidder having rights to publishing my fifty-plus years of data on the effects of yoyo diets. I could be their poster child for "This Will Happen to You—Without Us!" But then my skeptical mind convinced me that they would probably think the Petunia Pig binder was a hoax. And at some level, I wished that it were, and I was left with wondering whether I should hate or thank my skinny aunt. She died from heart disease two years before her then-chubby younger sister, my mother. And I am embarrassed to admit that this fact secretly tickled me, and I wondered if the irony occurred to Mom, too. Knowing Mom, probably not.

Back to my seven Borealis pounds. Time to get moving, I decided, and I had a plan. I became a wanderer, adding up steps and calories burned. I did this gradually. I started walking a circuit that included the hallways, the lobby, and the community room. Each round earned me five hundred steps, so my Fitbit reported. I did two rounds after every meal, walking like I was a drifter in search of goings-on. I kept a tight hold on my purse while walking, like Uncle Billy held on to his mega bank deposit in *It's a Wonderful Life*, and I also kept track of it as well as Uncle Billy did, still tending to leave it everywhere I stopped. So much more the effect, I rationalized, and I was relieved with the thought that at least I would not be walking into Sam.

One afternoon, while making my way through the lobby, I noticed Christine, who was always waiting hours too early for her granddaughter to pick her up for their weekly lunch date, tilting to the right, her walker in front of her. Why she picked the only armless chair at Borealis, I will never understand, but there she was like she was in suspended animation waiting for someone to holler "Timber!"

From about twenty feet away, I dashed to Christine's side and caught her just as her second cheek was leaving the seat cushion. As my arms locked around her abundant middle, I froze, scanning the room for witnesses of what I had done that I should not have been able to do.

Bear in mind, there were no dashers, no dancers, and no prancers at Borealis. I take that back—Gino could dance. He air-danced with an invisible woman he called "Marilyn," as in *the* Marilyn. But he knew she was invisible, so he could stay.

As luck would have it, a resident assistant, Denise, was at the front door standing behind the wheelchair of Carol, who was waiting for her son to take her to her great-granddaughter's violin recital. Carol could not even hear the earsplitting television in the community room—what were they thinking?

My eyes met Denise's, and I knew she had seen my moves. She stared at me like she was seeing me for the first time and could not place me. Still holding a by-then waking Christine, I gasped in sing-song, "Need some help here."

Denise left Carol and tended to Christine while I grabbed for a chair with fake trembling arms and fake wobbly legs and a *for real* shaky voice because I was thinking I had just blown my cover. I sat down as if I had just lifted the proverbial car off my child.

"Wow, Joni, those were some smooth moves you had there."

I let out another gasp. "Yeh, adrenaline, I guess."

She paused for a moment. "Oh, sure. Crap. That really works. I remember learning about that in school."

And all I could think was thank God she did not miss that class.

Denise told me to stay put for a while and that she would be back to take me to the nurse's office. And by the time Carol was well on her way to not hearing violin music and Christine was about to put in her order for sweet and sour pork, Denise escorted me to the "nurses' station" where the "nurse" took my blood pressure and pulse and offered me some Tylenol for the muscles she thought were surely soon to ache.

For the rest of the week, I took the Tylenol, less steps, and my time getting out of chairs. I made an extra effort to appear feeble and even more forgetful, again at least one other reason to be grateful for the absence of Sam. And the pounds stayed on . . .

Theories and Lists

While Sam was away, and my mind was missing the stimulation of cribbage and thought-provoking conversation, I started making lists. I have always been a list maker and I felt the need to identify commonalities, threads, and links among the residents. That is, without some form of organizational tool, the characteristics of the residents were coming together for me like a geometric string art design, blending and blurring. So I sought a means to experience those strings more separately, within the context of their individual wholeness, yet cross-referenced with their connectedness. Venn diagrams were always a favorite of mine, and my intent was to eventually put my lists into circles, the intersections of which I believed were sure to be revealing in some significant ways.

My first list was a birthday list (not what you think). I could care less about when their birthdays were or how old they were. I wanted to know whether they liked the idea of celebrating their birthday at Borealis, in traditional Borealis fashion. This list was born on Bert's birthday—Bert, the woman with a no-family family, the woman who deceived her lineage in not that different of a way than I was deceiving mine, me feigning senility, Bert feigning death.

At her dinner table, on the day that Bert turned eighty, she got a cake, a birthday hat, and everyone—staff and residents—singing, whether she wanted it or not. I didn't think she wanted it.

She looked ridiculous in that hat because that kind of hat goes with smiling, and she wasn't smiling. As I stood nearby and watched, the expression on Bert's face kept me from singing. It took me back to the Christmas when my mother told me she wasn't putting up a tree for the first time in the almost fifty years that I had known her. She didn't look sad or mad. She said it like she was telling me that she switched detergents. I recall holding back the comment, "You're getting old, Mom."

I then saw my old mother as regarding the happenings of the world with the dispassion of one condemned. In short, so what? Been there, done that. Why bother? Not worth the energy. Not going to be doing that much longer anyway. I did not see that my forever-fervent mother had redirected her passion from the shallows to the depths, finding the gold that had been buried within her, awaiting only wisdom. And *my* revelation, awaiting only mine.

That happened also to be close to the time when I was taking an online gerontology course, for continuing education credits to keep my nursing license and to prep for this project. I read a line in the course textbook that set me on fire for the duration of the course: "Older adults may enjoy a walk." Like they were another species! And I do believe that the on-fire part had much to do with the fact that the "they" was getting awfully close to being "me."

I looked at who was responsible for writing that drivel (the names will be held to protect the inane), and then I searched them online. And all four were under sixty, one under forty, and one, by god, barely thirty. And I ask you, how fair is that? Less fair than you are thinking right now, I predict, after you hear why I think it is unfair, not to mention inaccurate. Until then, contemplate that one of the many problems the old have has to do with the fact that the only ones studying and describing who we are, are not old, and never were old. This is very different from those who study the young, who at least were once young. Sort of like asking a caterpillar to analyze the flight pattern of a butterfly?

And accordingly, these books that tell us about how one ages well are written by the persons who, as they write, are doing everything they can to avoid becoming old. They cannot help it; it is the developmental stage in which they find themselves. Consequently, their message is that to age well we must *stay* active, *stay* sharp, *stay* connected, just like most of the writers of gerontology books are trying desperately to do, in their middle adulthood, where grey hair is dyed and faces are lifted. In other words, they write books that communicate the message that being a good old person equates with *not acting* like an old person. So, essentially, the old have no appreciable developmental level of their own, existing only in comparison to those younger. In fact, even the word these experts on aging have carefully chosen to describe us, "old*er* adults," sports a comparative ending that tells us that we exist only in relation to those younger than us. Because, heaven forbid, they would just plain call us "old."

Furthermore, the very word "stay" in those "stay active, stay sharp" phrases means to me that we would do well to remain as far from old as we can possibly get, perhaps wear a string of garlic around our necks as we face old age, or better yet, order some age-repelling kryptonite from that arrow-attached-to-a-smile company (I'm sure they must have it), which will arrive faster than the garlic will ever begin to work. In my view, however, the young and the old are more alike than either would like to believe—expressly that each *are* the other, only less so.

* * *

Relativity—Einstein defined this concept in 1905 as the dependence of various physical phenomena on the relative motion of the observer and the observed objects, especially regarding the nature and behavior of light, space, time, and gravity. In the case of who/what is old, I would additionally describe relativity as being dependent upon the *age* of the observer. We seem to understand this when it comes to beauty—that whole beholder's eye claim—but not when it comes to "old." Crap, even the word "only" in the line, "You are *only* as old as you feel," screams to us that old is where we never want to go.

And this is why I cringe when I hear that children in elementary schools are being traipsed off to nursing homes to visit the infirmed, dependent, and debilitated 4.2 % of old people who are institutionalized. This, I believe, just might be a set-up for these children to never find joy in their old age, learning to dread what they see, hear, and smell when neither their white nor grey matter is completely developed, and often not developed enough to compute that 4.2 percent statistic into perspective. In fact, the brain development of the young, especially relative to judgement and perceptions of teens, is an area of current study.

Accordingly, I wish to call for someone with more energy, more fluid joints, and more years left than I possess to conduct a retrospective study on the incidence of depression in the old relative to the nature of their exposure to the old in their early youth. I hypothesize that there will be a correlation. That is, unless these youngsters who visit nursing homes at an early age are/were provided with a proportional balance of exposure to the old who are not institutionalized, those well-intentioned adults may be doing them a serious disservice regarding their future ability to cope with their own aging. Therefore, for every 4.2 hours spent in nursing homes,

I contend that 95.8 hours should be spent in the company of the non-institutionalized old. Proportional representation is an important concept—some even wasted a lot of tea over it.

Potential retrospective researchers, you don't have to worry about interviewing the forgetful old about their childhood exposure to the 4.2 percent. First, we have great long-term memories (just don't expect us to remember you if you should need a follow-up interview), and second, if my hypothesis is correct, I maintain that a visit to a nursing home at a tender age, without proportional balance, will be embedded an inch deep into our cerebral cortices. I will get you started: I never visited a nursing home until I was in my fourth decade of life, and I am old and not depressed and I am finding joy in being old (most days). And an interesting fact about my first exposure to a nursing home, when I was both an adult and a nurse, is that I cried all the way home after that experience, which was how long it took me to put the then only 3.2 percent into *perspective.*

Decades ago, before I even conceived of this project, I was introduced to the concept of "perspective transformation," a theory of adult learning and resultant behavioral change first proposed by Jack Mezirow in 1978. His work sparked a plethora of professional reaction to his theory of transformational learning and, of course, as Jack likely intended, spin-off theories that tweaked this and that about his original posit.

I will attempt to provide a summary of Mezirow's concept, acknowledging the difficulty in capturing this complex theory in any such abbreviated stab. Mezirow begins with the premise that a defining condition of being human is that we need to understand the meaning of our experience, as in, "Why are we here?" Apparently, he must assume that mammals below us on the phylogenetic hierarchy do not do this, hence the "defining." Furthermore, for some persons, Mezirow states, any uncritically assimilated explanation of why we are here by an authority figure will suffice. But to *maximize* our learning, Mezirow claims, we must make our *own* interpretations, rather than merely act on the beliefs, judgments, and feelings of others. And transformative learning leads to this type of autonomous thinking.

Moreover, accepting that all persons are learners (because learning is life, he states) Mezirow said we change our beliefs, attitudes, and emotional reactions, which Mezirow calls "meaning schemes," by engaging in critical reflection. I call that soul searching. This change leads to perspective transformation. Perspective transformation explains how our sense of meaning changes over our lifetime, becomes transformed, influencing our thoughts and eventually our behavior, which includes our judgment and our choices. Seems like a "duh" now, but it wasn't back then—testimony to his influence.

When does this happen? Mezirow claims that perspective transformation usually results from a "disorienting dilemma," which is triggered by a life crisis or major life transition (e.g., a near death experience). He also states that it may result from accumulated transformations *over time*. And that sounds like aging to me. He does include the crises inherent in aging (relocation, loss of friends, ending a career) as examples of disorienting dilemmas, but I did not come across any claim that addresses that the overall developmental stage of aging, in and of itself, could be responsible for such a transformation.

In *Learning as Transformation* (Mezirow et al., 2000), Edward Taylor stated that "what we know about participants in the various studies is that they are mostly adults, usually between ages seventeen and seventy." He further discussed that questions are raised as to the role of transformative learning in the aging process. Seventy—not very far into old, these days, I dare say.

One aspect with which perspective transformation theorists differ has to do with *how* transformation comes about. Some claim this process is rational, analytical, and cognitive, using inherent logic. In other words, you know this is happening, you want this to happen, and you work to make this happen. Others claim, rather, that this change occurs intuitively, as an emotional process. In other words, it happens without us knowing it is happening, a part of personality integration.

From both my personal and professional unresearched perspectives, I happen to think it is a bit of both.

What does this theory have to do with my birthday list, and other of my lists? Consider my mother and her missing-in-my-action Christmas tree, and her demeanor related to that decision. Had she learned something about the celebration of Christmas that caused her behavior to transform? That her decision to go cold turkey treeless wasn't about losing her Christmas spirit in old age but rather about finding it, redefining it, transforming it—possibly to a higher level than mine, which had been assimilated by others, namely, Norman Rockwell and the Hallmark Channel?

And let's take another look at Bert, a mother who risked all to bring her family together. Bert appeared to me as though she did not want all the fuss over her birthday. But I should not assume that she didn't want the fuss any more than they should have assumed that she did, right? My point is that she should have been *asked*. If she were in her own home and someone came to her door on her birthday without being invited, she could have decided not to answer the door. But where was her door in that dining room at Borealis?

It reminded me of visiting hours at hospitals and nursing homes and assisted living facilities and rehab facilities, with which, as a nurse, I took and still take great issue. Imagine sleeping in your bedroom, and your neighbor comes into your home without even knocking and enters your bedroom with a "How-de-do?" There should be calls made to the patients, from the lobby, to request a visit, so the patient/resident at least has the time to wake up, get off the can, put in their teeth, comb their pillow hair, or say no. Some hospitals have such procedures, but *all* should. Better yet, the visitor should call from *their* home to the institutional room, which is now their friend's substitute home, and ask if the person is even wanting visitors at that time, or at all. I am aware that there *are* procedures, in some facilities, for restricting *all* visitors, but I am not talking about a complete restriction here. Perhaps I digress, but I do believe there is a connection here, namely, that we tend to assume people want what we want, especially when it comes to the old who we assume are too old to know what they really want.

Let's assume that I am correct about Bert not wanting that birthday gesture, and there is a big difference in someone wanting a gesture and someone appreciating a gesture, which in my sense was that she *did not* the former and perhaps *did* the latter. Example: I did not want the sixtieth birthday party my friend gave me, but I sincerely appreciated the gesture. With that assumption, would Mezirow say that Bert had transformed beyond such artificial displays of regard that are routinely done for all at Borealis, and in places like Borealis, and that what might have been more meaningful for her would have been a gesture by a few close residents to individually spend some additional time with her on her birthday? Or, perhaps more sensitively, no gesture at all but the offer of a celebration, which she could accept or decline?

With this in mind, I began to look differently at the gerontology book pronouncement that "older adults may enjoy a walk." My claim, better described as an exclaim, had been that it sounded to me like the authors were claiming we were another species. Well, Mezirow, thank you for helping me to see that maybe we actually *are* that different, and maybe it just takes someone close to our age, or more pointedly someone at our level of transformation, to understand that it's a good thing that we eventually see life differently, as in we are one up on our former selves. And one up on the selves who wrote that gerontology book who, by the way, cannot help it that they are not there yet. To them I say, "You are forgiven. I understand now." I still don't get their point about taking a walk, but I do grasp the concept that we are indeed different.

Let's take a final look at Mezirow's theory wherein he now lists (I am in good company) the phases of perspective transformation. My comments are in *italics.*

PHASES OF PERSPECTIVE TRANSFORMATION (My comments are in *italics.*)

1. Disorienting dilemma (*Recall he states this is not always the case, that it might be an accumulation of life events, like perhaps in aging, as I had previously mentioned.*)
2. Self-examination (*The degree to which this happens depends on where the person lies on the spectrum of those who subscribe to home-cooked thinking on one hand versus those who prefer take-out thinking on the other.*)
3. Sense of alienation (*Discomfort with one's former way of thinking—how I felt when my peers were duping Charlotte and I saw it differently, no longer feeling like I belonged in their sphere of knowing how to "handle" patients like Charlotte.*)

4. Relating discontent to others (*Me writing this book might be an example; I see this phase as a problem for the residents at Borealis, that is, finding someone who is transformed at their level to whom they can express their discontent, especially when most of their day-to-day disharmony is expressed to a much younger staff, not to mention just finding their words to express these thoughts and then finding the ears healthy and willing enough to listen.*)

5. Explaining options of new behavior (*Bert never even had a shot at explaining her need to avoid that birthday scene, if indeed my perception of her need was accurate.*)

6. Building confidence in new ways (*Not going to happen when shooting blanks in 4 and 5.*)

7. Planning a course of action (*Need 6—confidence.*)

8. Experimenting with new roles (*The prospective new roles have been rendered impotent by kryptonite and garlic. That is, we who are old dare not act so. "Get a damn Christmas tree, Mom."*)

9. Reintegration (*The old will die trying or try dying, before this occurs, in most cases. Again, we need to find someone to pay attention to us, to really listen to us.*)

Now, to be clear, again, Mezirow did not claim to be talking about aging, specifically, when developing this theory of adult learning. But if he believed life was learning, then would, should aging represent a person's ultimate level of learning? Certainly, there are psychosocial theories that do address aging specifically, that is, theories that take much of this into account. But the problem, for example, with nursing theories, with which I am most familiar, is that these theories must be proven, because nursing sees itself as a science (and an art, but the science is what holds us up here). Now, according to my take on this, how's that going to happen *accurately* unless the theorist/researcher waits until they are old enough to be transformed and unless they are injudicious enough to get themselves deceitfully admitted to a "nu—assisted living facility" while they still are capable of doing research? Otherwise, it is through the lens of one who has never been there developmentally, or bodily. And that, in my opinion, makes all the difference.

I am not a theorist. So, I ask the reader to simply take what I have to say and mull it over, not like you are on a dissertation committee, but rather like we are two people talking about old people, when at least one of us is old. That said, I know that even my perspective is partially skewed because I must admit to the feeling that I had throughout my stay at Borealis, that I was reading a book about myself and flipping ahead to see how it ended. Denial? Of course. But shh, don't tell me, lest I wake up believing I am old.

By my second week of making my lists, I had four. I originally had five, but I tossed out the "Happy" list, wherein I asked myself whether it appeared to me that the residents were happy. I realized that happiness could only be determined through *my* lens of happiness, and so how could I ever be able to know what happiness looked like for them?

The lists were as follows (and I admit that there is rarely an objective bone present in the bodies of these lists, but recall that their purpose was merely to help me organize my data):

Birthdays As stated earlier, this had to do with whether the resident wanted to celebrate their birthday in the customary Borealis cake-and-singing-after-dinner-with-a-paper-hat-on-your-head manner. I retrieved this info by simply rotating my dinner associates and mentioning casually, "I don't think I want to have a cake and singing in the dining room on my birthday" . . . and then I waited and listened.

Whose idea was their relocation to Borealis? From our conversations, I gleaned whether it was the resident's idea to live at Borealis, or someone else's, and this was not a difficult find about most residents because it was a frequent topic of discussion. This, I also found, seemed to have a significant impact on their attitude towards being institutionalized.

"Old" Some residents matter-of-factly referred to themselves as old. The fact that they said the word was objective, but, I admit, the "matter-of-factness" was totally subjective. That said, I could tell.

Transforming, yes or no? Now this was not so unlike the "Happy" list issue. However, happy is not on a continuum as transformation is; it is not developmental. But, for example, I felt I knew that Angie and Bert were transforming, but I could not even guess as to whether they were happy, and I sensed strongly that the Sylvia was neither transforming nor happy. My biggest problem was that this assessment was predicated on a continuum, as in we are all transform*ing* and we are never, ever, fully transform*ed*, so where did I draw the line? Brace yourself—I drew it at me, as in, was the resident more transformed than me or less? And I heard you: "How subjective is that?" Answer: It is very subjective, and you would not have asked that question if you were more transformed than me, so I just put you on the "not" side of that list.

My lists were not only helpful in keeping my thoughts straight, but also in guiding my discussions and observations. I found myself eager to get back to my room to debrief like never before. Accordingly, the lists were what I grabbed first because it beat the you-know-what out of a blank journal page. And, I amazingly had no trouble deciding who went on which list, except for Sam—the resident I was closest to…or was I?

Boyd, R. D., "Personal Transformation in Small Groups." 1991, New York: Routledge.

Mezirow, J. et al., "Learning as Transformation." 2000. Jossey-Bass Publishers.

Mezirow, J., "Transformative Dimensions of Adult Learning." 1991. Jossey-Bass Publishers.

Mezirow, J., "Transformative Learning: Theory to Practice." New Directions for Adult and Continuing Education, no. 74, Summer 1997, Jossey-Bass Publishers.

Donna

I was not getting good sleep since Sam was away. I did not even want to take a stab at fathoming the why behind that fact. I was not only having a hard time falling asleep, but also staying asleep, so I found myself one morning awake early enough for breakfast, for the first time ever since being institutionalized. Plus, I was hungry at that early hour when it had always been too early for me to be awake, let alone eat. I had gotten into the habit of having a protein bar, a piece of fruit, and coffee in my room, around ten, and so I usually was not hungry at eleven thirty when lunch was served. If I did do lunch, I rarely had more than a beverage and a cookie, sometimes soup. However, I put on the feedbag for dinner in a big way, and I snacked while I wrote at night. The story of my weight, for all my life.

The smell of eggs and pancakes made me lose my virgin breakfast hunger almost to the point of a needing-to-leave level of nausea. Getting away from where the aroma was intense helped, and so I found myself sitting in the television orbit with a cup of coffee and a banana. No one else was there, but the television was on, just in case. I guess I was the case. It was local news, and it reminded me of watching the news in Europe, with Jeff, during our Central Europe bus tour. It meant little to us, even when it was in English, because it was about another world, a world in which just traveling through on a bus did not help to make significant to us. And, similarly, *beyond Borealis* was another world as well. There it felt like I was disjointed from the mainstream, like I was watching a movie rather than a local news report. I wondered whether other residents felt the same, and if they did, why they were still so attracted to this news. Habit? Pretending to be connected? Another aspect to explore.

The dishes were no sooner off the table when Candice and Karen started to set up their Rummikub game. I had heard about their game, the fact that they kept count of the wins, and that they had broken the thousand game mark between them, with Candice taking only a slight lead. They had known each other since their daughters were young, serving together as co-leaders of a girl scout troop, as co-room moms, and on church committees. They had been playing this game against each other for decades, starting with the chaperoning of their first girl scout camp where they found themselves bored to death when the girls fell asleep too early for their internal clocks. It was the only game in the cabinet with all the pieces, they explained. The game eventually progressed to a foursome, including their husbands on weekly "hump day game days," and then reverted to a twosome when both became widows in the same year. I ate dinner once with them, during which I found them to be very pleasant and chatty. Maybe a little too chatty—hence this scoop, and hence the once. And there I go calling those kettles black, again.

I waited for them to get started and into the game before I approached. I wasn't familiar with the game and I wanted to see what it was all about. Sliding my bottom on the chair I had dragged over to them, I simultaneously slid my purse onto their table to get their attention. Purses got attention. Every table in that dining room had six chairs, which meant that these two ladies would have had to remove four chairs, a fact which should have served to forecast their eventual reaction to me, had I paid better attention. "I don't know this game at all. Mind if I watch?"

No answer. Chatty gone.

I said, a little louder, just in case that was the issue, "Good morning, Candice, Karen. Remember me, Joni Bohne? Mind if I hang out here and watch you play?" I leaned forward while talking and got in their field of vision, another just-in-case.

Neither hearing nor vision was the case.

Candice nodded to Karen and then tilted her head in my direction, sending her partner the message that I was there and needed to be dealt with, reminding me of Michael Corleone signaling for a hit. Alas, relievedly, no kiss, no fishing boat.

I really was not sure what was going on or not going on. Karen, eventually catching her commission, said to me, "Did you say something?" These words met my ears like I had just put my head into a freezer.

I repeated my request and she responded, "Sure," through a side-shifted mouth that looked like if I stuck a stogie in it, she could pull off a solid Edward G. Now more interested than ever, I pulled my chair closer to the table, causing Karen to put her arms around her tile rack full of tiles, shielding them from my sight, I guessed, in case I should get a notion to signal Candice. That made me smile. I love a true competitor.

I kept my eyes on the game and sensed I did not dare talk if I knew what was good for me, until I felt a tap on my shoulder. It was Donna wheeling by. She made her way to the wall on the opposite side of the room, swung her chair around, and then used her pointer finger to summon me.

As I left the ladies, I tranquilly but strongly said, "I have to go. Someone over there needs my kidney," and I waited, not long, for the reaction I was certain I would not get. And I was quite sure they never even noticed my retreat.

"You rang? Or I should say, you tapped?" I said to Donna.

"Yes, I was trying to save you," Donna said with a smile in her eyes and very little movement of her face. "You know, they aren't going to talk to you when they are playing that game. They don't even talk to each other."

"I kind of figured that, but thanks for telling me. At first I thought it was me."

"No, they just turned into men like most of us gals do here."

I pulled up a chair in front of Donna, crossed my legs, and folded my hands over my top knee in now-you've-got-my-attention fashion. She chuckled as she watched me deliver that message.

Donna was not much older than me, I guessed, but she had MS, and it had taken its toll. The first time we chatted she had told me she was diagnosed in her late forties and that she had the relapsing-remitting type of MS, "which was the best kind to have." Her legs, she had shared, became noticeably weaker in her sixties and she fell a couple of times, after which she tried a cane and then a walker, but balance issues eventually set her up with a wheelchair. And she made a point of saying she wasn't complaining, just explaining. She was a widow and used to "do hair" in her basement. She had traded a master's degree in international trade for a husband, five children, and a home salon. Donna had appeared on two of my lists by that time: she was on the "Yes" side of my transformed list, and I knew it was her idea to live at Borealis, "to spare her children," so she was on that list, also.

The MS had additionally affected the strength in her arms, sometimes causing her to double up on her hold of objects, but not enough to keep her from curling her hair with metal rollers, every morning, followed by sitting under a portable hair dryer that could be heard humming through the hall and into the community room. Explaining her perfect hair, she told me that her arms were stronger in the earlier part of the day. "Later in the day, I often feel "emessee," which at first sounded like she was saying "messy." She expelled a weak-on-the-outside but strong-on-the-inside laugh when I asked for clarification of messy. When I finally caught on to emessee, she expounded and told me it was an indescribable feeling, that the weakness of MS was not like any other weakness she had felt before her MS symptoms started appearing, not like flu weakness or fainting weakness, and that the same held true for the numbness and the headaches. People with MS were just using those words for lack of better words, she said, because there were no words for what they were really feeling.

I thought of all the MS patients I had cared for over my decades as a nurse, and I tried to recall their descriptions of their symptoms. I came up vacant and wondered why that was. Did I forget, or just never bother to listen? More likely, I pondered, I took for granted that their "weak" was my "weak," and that we all shared the same definitions for numbness and headaches.

"So tell me, please, Donna, about how I'm going to turn into a man at Borealis." I said this playfully, and Donna's spirit leapt to join my play date.

With a stifled laugh and a slipped snort, she replied, "Oh, it goes like this. You see, those gals are just singularly focused. It happens to all of us old people. But it's not a big adjustment for men, who were never able to multitask in the first place. It's a gender enhancement in our design—God needed to make women able to multitask so that they wouldn't go around losing all the children. Otherwise, what would be the point of all that going forth and multiplying? And men, of course, they had to focus, you know, hunting, fighting, working on a car, watching football. Couldn't have them distracted by kids or a baking pie during any of those tasks; no, that wouldn't do. But then when we women get older and there are no children to watch over, that part of us that makes us able to juggle all those tasks just disappears, because you know the saying, 'If you don't use it, you lose it.' So now, here, we all come together, singularly focused, and that's why you could drop a bomb in here and those two would never notice, and neither would Lyndon if he's watching Bonanza, or me if I'm setting my hair, or any of us women . . . if we can't place our purse."

I sat there in amazement, not so much of who she was, but of who I wasn't, to have missed her. I wondered if maybe she should be writing my book until I realized she was.

I found myself asking that question a lot since Charlotte: "Who I wasn't to have missed . . .?" Had I been their nurse, would I have missed Bert and Donna and Angie and Sam? I had the feeling the answer was yes. I had always spoken to the privilege of nursing, the privilege of being there for a person's best days (the birth of their children), and for their worst days (the diagnosis they didn't want). But what of the in-between privileges, the less glamorous everyday moments that revealed the person within? Was I there for those moments? And what would I have learned that I missed learning? Moreover, what else am I missing now? When my head hits the pillow of my death bed, will I still be asking, "Who I wasn't to have missed . . .?" And will the missed include not only my patients, but my family, friends, neighbors? Will I regret revering all too much that which kept me from being "who I wasn't to have missed"?

Oh God, say it won't be so.

That day, I was consoled by not missing Donna—and it was a start. "So, how and when did you come up with this theory of singular focus?"

"Oh, long ago. It's rare that I come up with new material these days. You see, hairdressers—I know they call them stylists now, la de da, are a lot like bartenders—we spend a lot of time ruminating on the nuances of life with our customers. And my customers were mostly women. And what do women like to do most when they are in a men-free zone, doing the woman thing while looking at themselves in a mirror, sort of like someone on a shrink's couch with no one looking back at them except themselves in the mirror? They talk about men. Well, mostly they make fun of them. So, you see, I can't take full credit for this revelation. It developed over many years and many tears, some of joy, some not so much, some of mine, some of theirs." She readjusted herself in her wheelchair saying, "Gotta shift the lead, or it turns red." Then she folded her hands on her lap and asked, "So what's your story, lady?"

I was tempted to disclose to her more than I had to anyone at Borealis, including Sam, but I held back. "Nothing exciting, Donna. Been there, done that. Now I'm being here, doing this."

A snorty snicker led to, "I like that. Quite illusive. Oh my God, where's my purse?" She patted her wheelchair aside each leg, feeling frantically for her purse, or so I thought, until she added, "Just pulling your chain, sweetheart. I'm not there yet. But check me out next week." She made a chair swing like she was going to pull off an exit and then she concluded our visit with, "Time for Bingo. Coming?"

I joined her for Bingo, and later that day, 50 cents poorer, I added Donna to my "Old" list because she talked about being old like my mother did, rather pragmatically. Listening to her, it seemed like a good place to be, but I was not there yet. I was only where I wrote about other people talking about it or not talking about it.

He's Back

During the week that Sam was gone, I spent a lot of effort on convincement of the staff, as in asking staffers often if Sam had returned, and then acting like he had never left and that I couldn't find him. And then I would remember, "Oh that's right, he is staying with his daughter." It was my golden opportunity to make headway on this task, with Sam away and unable to witness my fake decline. But I was careful not to inch beyond "cute and forgetful," lest I cross that Borealis "cut" line in the sands of my time left there. For Borealis assessed my behavior with long-term in *their* minds.

On the day that Sam was scheduled to return, I felt like I was pregnant with Andy, nauseated beyond cracker relief. I wasn't quite sure why I was so worried. Was it that he might be returning for just an interim, before permanently relocating? Was it that his doctor appointment might have been revealing in some way that was not good? Was it that I was wondering if he missed me as much as I missed him? Or was it something else tucked under a veil of denial?

Having no idea what time of day Sam would be arriving, I was not sure where I should place myself to receive him, if in fact he was to be received, by me. I toyed with whether to stay in my room and hope he would seek me out versus hang out in the community room like I was just waiting for our card game. Undecidedly, I did both—waited in my room in the morning and stayed in the community room after lunch.

I was reading the *Readers' Digest*, using earplugs to drown out the blaring television, when I felt a tap on my shoulder. And there he was.

I dropped the *Digest* and practically jumped into his arms for a hug. We had never hugged before and I certainly had not planned that, but I felt invited by his facial expression and his posture. When he hugged back, hard, I heard a couple of "aww" s in the background and I didn't care who in the hell it was. I was just so glad to see Sam that nothing else mattered.

As we pulled apart, I looked behind him for Tammy, and he read my mind, "She left."

And as spontaneous as that greeting was, was as awkward as my next move felt. Gentleman that he was, he came to my rescue, adjusting my chair and guiding my shoulders to sit back down. Then he slowly sat in the chair across from me, as if using the time to plan *his* next move. Surveying the room, he saw that we were attracting more attention than *Wheel*, and he quickly changed course, "Let's go for a walk?"

He looked different, or was it that he was acting differently? His facial skin appeared looser. Weight loss? More relaxed? He had always been calm, but this was a deeper calm, perhaps resigned? The nurse in me wondered if this tranquility meant a change was coming that Sam had finally accepted, or did it mean that some prescription had kicked in?

His pupils were normal-sized. His breathing seemed slower and deeper than I recalled, but then again, we weren't playing cards. He looked less "Ronny," probably because of the haircut, I reasoned.

The rest of his body looked the same. I couldn't put my finger on it. I wanted very much to get past the openers and announce, "Play ball." *Be patient*, I told myself, like that ever worked.

We walked in silence, me not knowing what to say, Sam appearing to have a plan, a destination. He stopped us at one of the staff offices and told me he would be just a minute; I had no idea why. One of the administrators followed him out of the office and then lead us to the Family Dining Room. Unlocking the door, "Just let me know when you're done, Sam."

The "FDR," as it was ironically called in that ultra-conservative area, was a large room that contained a twenty-foot table in its center and several wall-hugging loveseats that snuggled up to end tables that held lamps much too big for them. All the lamps at Borealis were oversized for their footings—probably the better-to-see-with those large lamps, and the better-to-navigate walkers and wheelchairs with those smaller tables that occupied less floor space.

The walls were painted blue, but that was the wrong color for what was most definitely Borealis' ultimate "green room." That is, though the room was designed to be reserved by residents when they wanted to have a private dinner with their family, the only time I saw it being used was when Borealis hosted a health fair for the community, the very community that contained its likely future residents.

On that autumn health fair day, blood pressures were taken, hearing and vision was screened, and finger prick samples were tested for blood sugar and cholesterol. All of this was market-timed before the arrival of the potential harsh winter that just might unleash the straw that would break those living-alone elders' backs—the planting of the seed, so to market.

In preparation for the fair, residents were handpicked to be greeters and to pass out cookies and freebies, such as "Borealis" pill organizers and magnifiers. Borealis also handpicked residents who needed to be "occupied" in the exercise room, where the long narrow door window was covered from the inside and the sign on the outside read "Do not Disturb. Class in Session." Bert was one of the residents slated to be "occupied" in that "class" on that day. I was among the chosen who were asked to assist, and I requested the cookie detail so that I could move around and check out the scene *while* eating kolacky. They invited Sam, most likely to showcase his charming daytime normalcy, but he declined their invitation and spent the day in his beige room.

But there was no health fair on that early spring day when Sam corralled me into the FDR for a talk. "We can talk in here, without the *Wheel* and without the *Wheel* watchers," Sam said in a very kind way, not like he was putting down the rubberneckers, but rather like he was charmed by them. I thought about how much nicer of a person he was than me—I was ready to flip them the bird. But then again, he had been away from them for a while.

We sat next to each other, in armchairs at one end of the long table. My heart was racing, and I wondered whether his was.

"Sam, how are you?"

"I'm good, Joni. I'm better. I saw a new neurologist, again. She's trying me on a new sleeping pill that she hopes will keep me asleep at night. How about you?"

That was the most he had ever talked to me about his episodes of delirium, but he changed the subject rather quickly. Was that because he wanted the subject changed, or because he was being polite asking about me? "I am fine. Miss our card games, for sure."

"I missed more than the card games," he said very seriously, leaning closer. Damn, I felt the rush of blush, and damn if he didn't notice.

"Me too. Sam, are the sleeping pills working?" I really wanted to ask if Borealis gave him a ticket for a ride down the road, but we weren't there yet.

"Well, sort of. Now I sleep longer before I turn into Chucky." He smiled a sad smile and half-reached for my hand. "Actually, I did have fewer episodes, but I always have fewer episodes away from here. And they weren't as bad, as in I didn't break anything or anybody, so I guess that's progress." He arched backwards and looked up at the ceiling, exhaling a deep sigh. "This is about the fifth prescription from now the third doctor. So, what's been happening around here?" Another change of that subject.

I took time to think. "Not much. Oh, that's right, Arnie took on the Bingo bi—lady." He laughed harder than I have ever heard him laugh, harder than I had ever heard Jeff laugh. I wondered if he was laughing about Arnie or about me stopping myself from saying "bitch".

"Arnie's the bomb."

Silence.

We stared at our hands, separate, on the table, all four of them longing to connect. I decided to wait him out.

Finally, he said, "Joni, there is something I have to tell you." His voice squeaked and the muscles in his face seeped into abandon. "About Birch." He gave another sigh and bit his lip. "But first I want to let you know that Tammy told me how you stopped her when she was about to tell you about the accident. She told me why, too. That's a lot o' class, Ace. I appreciate that loyalty." He took in a slow deep breath, like he was trying to calm himself. "But it's time I told you."

That "time" part chafed. "It's *time*, Sam?" I searched his eyes for the why behind his decision to disclose. I would not allow it to be that he owed me, that he felt obligated.

He shook his head ever so slightly like he was erasing his last statement. "I *want* to tell you." I loved that he caught my rub, as subtle as I thought I was being. He examined my yet-pensive stare, and tried again, "I *need* to share this with you, Joni."

"Go ahead, Sam, I'm listening." I felt like a shrink saying that, and I hoped he didn't think so.

He tried to settle himself with breathing and position adjustments. I had never seen him look so out of sorts except, of course, during his night spells. He fixed his gaze on our hands, still apart, but barely. I could not help but notice that our hands looked like they could have gone through the same life, in terms of wear and tear. Like mine and Bert's. Like mine now and my mother's then. I tried to picture what Jeff's hands would have looked like now.

Picturing Jeff now? Why? I wondered.

He started, finally, using an uncharacteristic staccato delivery and cadence, like a telegraph message minus the "stops," like he had told this story many times before. "It was Birch's golden birthday. He was fourteen on that January 14. Every birthday, usually on or very close to his birthday, he and I went ice fishing." Sam's eyes met mine, and he knew I knew where this was going. And oh, damn—I just then remembered that once, while playing cards, I had told Sam the story about my cell phone going into the lake through an ice hole, like it had nearly ended my world.

Sam continued, seemingly oblivious to my embarrassment, making no eye contact, looking downward as if reading from a script. "It was a warm day in January, thirty-five degrees, January thaw. We decided to take the ATV out to the icehouse. We went out after dinner, after birthday cake. We missed flags that alerted bad ice. We hit a ridge and had to back up off the ridge, and we backed up into a small stretch of slush. We got stuck there, and within what seemed like a moment we went down. The ATV went down to the right, and I was driving, so while it yet hung on the edge of the ice momentarily on my side, I got off the ATV and made it to a slab of solid ice. Birch was underwater. I ran around to his side and tugged on his foot—all that I could reach from the ice. But he wasn't budging, and he wasn't moving, so I jumped in. I never should have done that because I couldn't release Birch from the ATV while in the water. Then it took me too much time to get myself back on ice—time Birch didn't have. I found out later that Birch's overalls were hung up on the ATV. I was screaming and pulling. I still had only his foot. Even if I had known he was hung up, I had nothing to even attempt to cut him loose with. I was shivering violently and losing strength. I panicked. When someone showed up to help us, he cut Birch free, but it was too late. We tried CPR. He hadn't been moving because he was knocked unconscious when his head hit the ice under the ATV." Sam continued to sit stiffly, but closed his eyes at that point, and suddenly it came clear to me why Sam had picked "Old Maid" for a "ya-ya game" reference, rather than "Go Fish," during that very first time we met.

I cupped my hands over his. "Oh Sam, I am so sorry."

After a couple of deep breaths, a more relaxed but weary Sam proceeded, but now in his usual, casual, Sam tone, "He didn't even want to go fishing that day. He wanted to go to his friend's house.

But when I showed disappointment—well, he was that kind of kid—he acted like he would rather go with me, even though I knew that wasn't the case. And to ease my guilt about taking advantage of him not pushing the issue of going to his friend's, I told myself that he'd be better off with me because I didn't like the friend he wanted to hang with. *Better off with me . . .*" Sam trailed off and broke down. "He was a good kid, Joni, gentle, smart, funny. He looked a lot like your Andy."

I stood and moved my chair closer to Sam and held him while he sobbed, and then I fished the belly of my shirt out of my bibs to wipe his face. I kissed his forehead curls aside. Those chairs were so small, so hard, that I looked at the carpeted floor with the thought of moving us there, but I doubted whether we would ever get back up without help. I moved again, to sit on his lap, one foot pushing up on the floor to lessen my weight on his septuagenarian legs, and I laid my head on his still-broad-but-yielding chest. And when I heard voices in the hallway, I felt like we were two teen lovers listening for the sound of parents who were getting all too close.

We sat for a few minutes in silence and I could feel his chest quaking as he held back a torrid sob. He then stroked my hair and continued, "Jane never forgave me. I could tell, even though she did everything possible to convince me otherwise. She never liked the idea of ice fishing. She only went ice fishing once and when the water level rose and fell in the holes as a truck passed by, she hit the floor and screamed for me to get her out of there. I knew she felt I put our son's life at risk for a few fish dinners, because she had always used that line before the accident when she tried to discourage us from heading out. I had let her down in the worst way a husband can let down a wife—killing her child."

I whispered as I squeezed his hand, "Oh Sam, you didn't kill him."

"If I had a dollar for every time I told myself that, Joni, I'd have enough dollars to buy everyone here a steak dinner. But unfortunately, if I had the same dollar for every time I told myself I killed him, I could buy everyone here a whole damn cow." He adjusted us in the chair, probably because his legs were falling asleep under my weight, and then he added, "And Birch's death is not the only death I am responsible for, because I truly believe grief was what caused Jane to get sick. Her grief and her suppressed anger towards me acted like a vitamin for her gluttonous cancer. After Birch died, I tried to be the best husband I could imagine any man being, and now I regret that effort. I should have been a bastard, and then her body would have revved up against me and readied her for her fight against those aberrant cells that set up camp in her unarmed, vulnerable body. She could have left me and moved on, healthy."

Sam's face . . . I had never seen a face so sad. Not even when I looked in the mirror and for the first time saw a widow looking back. Laugh lines deepened to trenches, lids slumped over eyes that begged to be shielded from the eye contact that would only make it worse. This expression of Sam's was a stranger to me, or was I a stranger to it? I had seen Sam serious, relaxed, playful, and even anguished at night. Had I missed his sad face while melding high? Oblivion? Like swallowtails lighting on road scat, unaware of the approaching tire that will make it their last meal. No. It just could not be that I would not have seen this face that screamed sad. It just could not be that I would not see it for the pain it messaged. Not possible.

Oh God, again, please say it isn't so.

Forty-plus years a nurse and I could not think of a damn thing to say. Even if I could, I would not have been able to say it because my throat felt like there was a rock lodged in the back of it and my parotid glands were feeling mump-like. I never felt so bad and so good, at the same time.

Finally, after maybe a solid five minutes of body-numbing inertia, a timid knock on the door set us into motion. I moved quickly to my chair like a kid caught, and Sam sat up straight and managed, "Yes?"

"Sam, it's Kay, just checking if you're still in there."

"We are," he said, while making his way to the door. He opened the door enough for Kay to see that we were dressed and upright. "We'll be out in a few," he said, languidly.

I felt frustrated by the fact that we were at the mercy of a thirty-something to have this moment together. I felt like asking her if the key hanging from her neck was her skate key. Here we were two mature adults and we had to carve out an opportunity for us to share privately, in someone else's house. And for the first time at Borealis, I felt like a prisoner, like the guard was on the other side of the door with the news that visiting hours were over. I reminded myself that this was my doing, but then I looked at Sam and that lingering question of why he was there to have to go through this gnawed right through any sensitivity I had, causing me to blurt out through partially clenched teeth, in restrained agony, "Sam, why are you here?"

He appeared stunned, as if wondering "Where did that come from?" And then he looked at the door, and he knew. "She didn't mean anything by that. I told her we'd only be a short—" And before he could finish his thought, I blurted again, like I was holding back a scream, "You do not need to be here. You should be your own man in your own home. Why are you here?" And why I started crying still baffles me to this day, but I could not have stopped it if I had wanted to—my cry took on a life of its own. This lack of control was disturbing to me for I was always in control of my emotions . . . before Sam? Before being old?

Sam came close and hugged me. "I at least have the crazies at night. What's your excuse for being here, Ace?"

I know this would be hard for any reader to believe, but I had never given that turn a thought. I figured I had given the staff and my family ample reason to verify my need for placement at Borealis, and until then I had not considered that I never showed that behavior to Sam, even though I knew I was restricting my antics in his presence. Odd, but true. There must be a defense mechanism in there somewhere.

And, alas, I am embarrassed to admit that this is the reply that came out of my mouth, "I asked you first."

I wished I had not asked. The answer was painful. Sam decided, shortly after Jane died, that he would enter an assisted living facility when he turned seventy-five, whether he needed it or not. The reason, he added, was that he wanted to ease the worries of Tammy who would bear all the burden of her father's "rusty years" without help from a brother and a much-younger-than-her-father mother, both of whom would likely have been alive and there for her "had it not been for the poor judgment of her father." Tammy originally fought him on that decision, but he felt quite certain that she not only had adjusted but was experiencing the relief he had planned for her, especially considering the development of his nocturnal chapters. Sam said he never wanted to expose Tammy, her husband, and their three children to his episodes, and both he and Tammy felt that Sam living alone was not a good option either.

When I commented that I had not seen his grandchildren at Borealis, he said he had asked Tammy to go along with the story that he had moved to his vacation home in Texas, that without knowing about his night terrors, even at their young age, they would have questioned his need to be at Borealis. When the time was right, he said, they would tell them that he was just then going to move in to Borealis. Sam's father was born in Houston, explaining his Texas connection, his name, and his Skype backdrop—me palm trees, and he cacti.

When the time came for my turn, I panicked. I hate to use that word after Sam used it about the death of his child, but no other word in my or Roget's lexicon seems to capture the feeling quite right. Maybe "panicked light." I had planned to tell Sam eventually about the real me, and that moment would have been the perfect opportunity—two people who were here for the benefit of others is how I would couch it. But, somehow, at that point, my reason paled so in comparison to his that I could not bring myself to disclose. But if I didn't tell him the truth, what would I tell him? That I was mildly confused most of the day, except when I was with him? The absurdity aside, I could not lie to him—to just about everyone else, but not him. However, I must admit that the list of people I was having trouble lying to was rapidly multiplying. Accordingly, I was beginning to realize I did not have what it takes for such research, for if I told him nothing, would he have thought I didn't trust him enough to confide in him? I could not chance that, project notwithstanding. I knew I had to tell him soon. I had only nine weeks left. Once again, I felt like the fly in the proverbial tangled web, only Sam was no spider—he would free me if he noticed my struggle.

I then did something I never expected myself to do—I told the truth. Well, not the whole, actual truth about why I was there, but the truth about not being sure whether I could tell Sam the truth, then and there. It went something like this: "Sam, I'm going to ask you to trust me on this. I can't talk about why I'm here right now because I'm not sure if it's the best thing to do. I need time." I would have been so pissed if he had said that to me, but Sam did not seem to be bothered, perhaps, I thought, because he no longer felt he had the right to be upset with anyone ever again. And one would think that his letting me off the hook on that quagmire of an explanation would have made me feel relieved, but no, because then I had to worry about whether I meant enough to him to even get him pissed in the first place.

It was another *"Poor Jeff"* moment. How did he do it, and for so long? I must have been a total piece of work for a wife.

Oh Deer, Dear!

The weeks moved slowly into spring, during which time the complexion of Borealis changed as I guessed it commonly did in all such facilities, considering the admission ticket for a room there was a deficit of one sort or another. For, at those ripe ages, deficits propagated exponentially, and thus residents left and new residents came—spring migration.

Angie had another stroke and was reduced to mumbling numbers that did not add up to much, and relocation efforts were quickly set into motion—she would never return to Borealis.

The resident who replaced Angie was a feisty sort, and she teamed up with Sylvia to jointly give Arnie the verbal "what for" s on a daily basis, causing his retreat from the community room while grumbling, "This is bullshit." When this happens to kids, it is called bullying; when it happens to adults, bullshit?

Whereas all of this bullying/bullshit occurred seemingly unnoticed by staff, the residents were most definitely in the know, but they didn't dare challenge Sylvia, much less her untested acerbic sidekick, and furthermore, they justified, Arnie was about due for his comeuppance.

Sam was still experiencing his nocturnal episodes of delirium and with unaccountable increasing frequency, as snow and ice melted, and birds returned.

Bert fell during a heart attack and was put on hospice at Borealis (per her Living Will), dying eight days later with only myself and a hospice volunteer at her side. Her children had visited, separately, and I presumed that was coordinated, not coincidental. Not one of the three of them had any intention of seeing her through to her end. Each had made that clear to both me and staff, nonverbally, as I sat unobtrusively next to her. I would quietly leave her room shortly after each of them arrived, respecting their need for a private moment to say they were sorry. Her daughter asked a staffer, like I wasn't there, who in the hell I was. When I answered, "Her friend," I surprised myself at how proud I was of that fact.

I was pleasantly surprised when Borealis allowed me to stay with Bert during her final hours but figured they probably decided better benign, confused me than no one, for I was the resident who was closest to Bert at Borealis. Up to that point, I had been sitting with Bert every evening for at least a half hour, even though we rarely spoke to each other. We just spent time together, and I believed that she liked it because she rarely lifted her head except at 7:00 PM when she was expecting me. Once I sang to her. I decided she didn't like my singing, because when I asked her the next evening if we should sing (even though she had not joined), she did not lift her head, change her expression, or make a sound. And I could just tell it was not doing anything for her. I can admit that I do not have much of a voice—a very limited range, but I love to sing. At least now I asked.

She died with her hand in mine. And she was the one who reached for that to happen.

* * *

Minnesota springs are noted for the type of weather that the rest of the country calls winter. So, while we at Borealis rarely had an opportunity to sample the proverbial spring in the air that once accompanied the spring in our steps, the season was brought inside as excitement centered around the residents starting indoor seed-lings that were kept on tables along the full-windowed west wall of the community room. That, I liked. We planted mostly flower seeds, annuals, that would eventually be planted in the abundant flower beds scattered across the Borealis campus. And lots of tomato plants. Signs of life and growth were otherwise rare to come by at Borealis, unless we're talking tumors and moles and hair where it never before had grown.

I was always just turning over for my last stretch of shuteye when the morning watering was taking place most days, but I made sure I got in on the late afternoon sprinkle. Throughout the day there were always a few residents leaning over the little plantlets. Their puffballs of white hair glistened baby blue under the ceiling-hung grow lights, and they would sit there on their walker seats with their hands clasped across their chests, just watching, as if they might catch those sprouts reaching. For as long as some of them would sit there, I thought that maybe they did.

One afternoon, after cribbage, Sam and I walked to the win-dow to look at the wall of plants that presented a sharp contrast to the early spring storm that had been dumping wet and heavy snow on the other side of the window. Having been an entomologist and choosing Birch and Tamarac for his children's names, I figured Sam to be a plant expert, and he did not disappoint. That, and the fact that I learned that he had his own greenhouse, made me certain that this would be a trip worth taking. As we surveyed the seed-lings, Sam was quiet at first, but when I told him I wished I knew more about plants, he took the podium. To say the least, he was not limited to what was on the back of the seed packages. Autotropism, alternation of generations, internodes, and petioles came flying out of his mouth like from John Coffey's in *The Green Mile*. I should have been clearer—I was mostly interested in what color they would be. But it was refreshing to see Sam confident and engaged in front of the very window that so often stole his soul during so many horrific nights. It felt so right to be standing there, next to him, like we were at a conservatory, like he was the tour guide. It felt so wonderfully "not Borealis."

But then so right turned so wrong. Lyndon, at the other end of the long line of tables, yelled out, "The deer! She fell in! She fell through the ice!" Everyone who could run, ran to the window—that would have been staff. The rest made their way to the wall like a tsunami of wheelchairs, walkers, and rapid-tapping canes which ended with the plants getting high on an overdose of carbon dioxide.

The staff and the residents began buzzing about what to do, whom to call. The deer was swimming in a circle of open water smack dab in the middle of the pond, trying to catch hold of the ice's snowy edge, stopping every so often, tired. It looked like she had been struggling for some time, the way she was taking breaks. Apparently, her dew claws were not gaining her the traction she needed to alley-oop.

Somebody suggested calling the DNR. *They probably don't have the proper equipment*, I thought, and even if they did, by the time they would get it together, the doe would be dead—the DNR not being known for their minute-men capabilities. But I remained quiet, resisting the urge to take charge, because I really shouldn't have been able to think that quickly or that sharply.

When the doe almost made it onto the ice, giving it all she had, a harmonic high-pitched "Ohhhhh" was heard, which then transitioned into a low-pitched "Uhhhhh" when she fell back in. That was it. I couldn't take it. I had to tell them to call the fire department, my cover be damned.

Staring ahead, facing the window, I started with a subliminal consciousness-tapping mantra, "Fire department. Fire department." Then I said it a bit louder, and again louder. And it worked. I heard someone else pick up on my chant and yell, "Call the fire department!" I looked up at Sam to check for his reaction, wondering if he caught on to what I was doing, and then I caught *him*.

His tall body, arched into an upper case "C," was descending slowly to his right, towards me, like a slinky navigating a final stair. A rusty slinky. I grabbed his upper arm, stretched my right leg as far back as I could and guided him to slide down the left side of my body, a safe-fall move I had been taught and used dozens of times in my nursing career.

Sam made it rather indelicately to the floor, considering the dramatic encounter of our combined arthritic joints. Certainly, the descent was not quite the "smooth waltz" I was taught to aim for in nursing school—ours was more like a cha-cha-cha. Cradling Sam's head at my left shin, I stuffed a sweater (that some thinker handed me) under his heavy head. I was looking at Sam's face, upside down to mine, and if that wasn't scary enough as it always is, his chalky face and blue lips caused me to not even notice the droplets of his sweat that had found my face in all the jarring.

I never said a word until he was safely on the floor, singularly focused as the man I was becoming, and then with a shake of his shoulders, "Sam, what's wrong? Sam? Sam?" He was unresponsive. His face drained from beet red to a sick gray in seconds and his hand was ice cold, like hundreds of hands I had held waiting for the morgue cart to arrive. That damn puffed-up Packers sweater made it difficult to determine whether he was breathing. If he was, it was very shallow. I put my hands to my face, in the combined horror and panic of not knowing what to do next, and it was then that I felt Sam's sweat on my face, certain it wasn't mine because I had always had a dry stress response. And then I felt intense pain in my knees—bone on bone—I thought adrenaline was supposed to take care of that.

Where was everyone who should be helping? Oh, crap, I finally realized, they were knee-deep in doe rescue efforts. I raised up on one knee (ouch) to look out the window and saw the heads of three of our five total staff members standing along the pond's shore. The others were likely on the phone or, being a Saturday, cleaning rooms with earbuds blasting rap. I yelled for someone to get help. I felt for Sam's pulse, but my hand was shaking so hard that I knew I wouldn't have felt it if he had one. I put my hand lightly over Sam's mouth and nose and thought I felt air flowing, but I wasn't sure. Damn, I wasn't sure about anything. Where was that capable nurse I had been? Sam's life was literally slipping through my incompetent hands, and no one, except for the sweater person who was then nowhere to be found, had been paying any attention to the two of us.

I attempted another shout-out but was drowned out by a con-glomerate of shrieks announcing, "Dennis is outside!" Dennis was a resident. When the remaining two staffers heard that news, wherever the hell they had been, they bolted through two different doors to get to him before he fell on the driveway. No, Dennis was not trying to save the doe, nor trying to escape. Dennis was braving the storm in his accountant wingtips, with no coat, no gloves, and no hat, to clear the snow off the sideview mirrors and the license plate of the main-tenance truck that had been plowing the driveway, but which was by then halted for the rescue.

Even BB, Dennis was known to have an idiosyncrasy of need-ing to clear snow off signs, mainly highway and street signs. As one would guess, such weather, when signs were obliterated by snow, did not make for the best time to pull over to the side of the road, so Dennis had always been prepared with a trunk filled with all his snow service needs—flares, shovels, a long-handled broom, and knee-high boots.

Arnie once told me that Borealis moved their "No Parking" sign from one end of the circular drive to the other to prevent Dennis from seeing it from the community room window, which would likely prompt his need to clear it. Arnie explained Dennis' eccentricity this way: "It's like when someone needs to straighten a crooked-hanging picture or scratch an itch—just drives him crazy 'til the sign is cleared." Arnie paused and shook his head like he just couldn't figure, and added, "You'd think a guy like him would have found a home south." I loved Arnie.

After Arnie's disclosure regarding Dennis, I had arranged to score the anomalous experience of eating supper with Dennis—the men copped this particular table early and so there was rarely a seat available, much less one available for a woman. I acted gen-der unaware, putting their polite to a test, and they passed. I chose that particular day to break gender ranks because it was snowing, which afforded me the lead-in to perhaps discuss Dennis' obsession with sign-clearing. I told my story about directing traffic during a snowstorm when the traffic lights were nonfunctional, hoping he would relate. And, during the story, I could not help wondering if I would be Dennis at Borealis one day when I really did need to be at Borealis. Dennis looked like he might be connecting, never taking his eyes off me during the telling, yet he did not offer any comments or nonverbal cues that would positively support my storm service.

I was hoping he might disclose an experience, perhaps an accident, which had triggered his need to keep signs visible. But Lyndon *did* pipe up with, "Dennis clears signs in storms," and a couple of others at the table chuckled, but Dennis said nothing, redirecting all his attention to his nearly empty plate, and so I was left still wondering.

I guessed Dennis had "too-old-to-have-been-diagnosed Asperger's," though I never heard as much, for Dennis would jump at the chance to answer a call-out question posed during the news, standing in front of the group as if at a lectern, explaining away in accurate detail such topics as the US history related to Russia and Syria, the definition of recession, the difference between a hurricane and a tornado. During these recitations he made no eye contact, moving his eyes slightly left to right like he was reading from an invisible book. And he was largely ignored.

Conversely, he very pointedly avoided small talk with small groups like the rest of us avoided constipation. In such venues, he fidgeted and squirmed until he figured a way out. And he always did, within short minutes.

I didn't know why Dennis was at Borealis—retired accountant, widower, father, appearing able-bodied and able-minded, except for the snow-clearing preoccupation. *Yet another book?* I mused. And the semblance of a cast of elders, with feigned age impairments, in so many "nu—assisted living centers," across the globe, writing the same book, would one day tickle my inners. But not that day.

So there, on that traumatic afternoon, was the Borealis staff, half on doe duty, the other half on Dennis duty. As they ran to Dennis, apparently he anticipated their intentions were to keep him from his mission, and in response he accelerated his pace. And he slipped. And he fell, all six-foot, two-hundred-plus pounds of him.

The inside residents, having cracked the window to hear the conversations accompanying the doe and Dennis saves, heard the staff admonishing a downed, laughing Dennis so: "It's not funny, Dennis!" Maybe it wasn't Asperger's, I later reckoned—shouldn't he have been anxious? Or maybe it was an anxious laugh. OCD? Maybe both? We knew so little about each other, and I began to reason that we were all in one great conglomerate state of denial—don't ask, don't tell, so that we are not asked and we don't have to tell, if we even knew. Perhaps not knowing was just a good place to be in our Borealis world.

In all the commotion, Sam and I were invisible and inaudible. First, because of the trifecta of traumas, and second, because the only eyes and ears left in sensory shot were hard of seeing and hearing.

Hoping to see someone, anyone, who might assist us, I again swiveled my neck and scanned the room, arthritic exorcist-style, the room that then seemed twice as large and one hundred times as empty as it had seemed just moments earlier. But still no one was coming forward; no one even looked like they *could* or *would* come forward. Running out of "appropriate-for-a-nu-assisted-living facility" swear words and the patience to find them, I said it, like I was sorry, but that I had to say it, "F---!"

The sound of me uttering that word stunned me into action, because the truth was that I had only said that word in the earshot of another twice before in my life: when I found a lump in *my* breast, and when I found Jeff, alongside me in our bed, with *his* not rising. Now, it wasn't that I was too pure or noble for that utterance, but rather in my youth, I was too afraid to say it aloud for fear of my life forever changing in ways I did not want it to change. And, in my adulthood, having learned what the word meant and near to the same time learning that what it meant was something just about everyone wanted to do, it seemed inappropriate to use it to express contempt. Might as well say, "Get hugged."

I got behind Sam to set up for rescue breaths and CPR, and as I positioned my lips over his, he jerked his head forward and vomited. Now, by this time, I had experienced many accidental body fluid encounters as a nurse, but this was the only one that actually smelled and tasted good, because it meant that the man that I loved was still alive.

With that news, I found my voice and my confidence. I screamed for someone to turn off the television that was competing with my dry, waning voice, and then I screamed for someone to help me turn Sam to his side. A pubescent environmental services staffer appeared and reluctantly joined me for the log roll of Sam, only after I changed my request to an order. Once side-lying, I inserted my fingers into Sam's mouth to sweep out the lunch chunks and Sam did not like that—go figure—and he woke up. He woke up! He used every facial muscle he had to pry open his salted, jellied-closed eyes, and then in less than the time it took me to use my sleeve to wipe his partially digested lunch off my face, that masterful mind of his took in the situation, and he managed to utter in a very weak and deliberate voice, which only myself and my log rolling partner could hear, "You need to learn how to take your cribbage losses without getting violent, Ace." And then he passed out again. Forty-plus years a nurse and I had never witnessed any patient coming out of a faint using humor.

And the good news was that the fire department was there already, for the deer, by the time the adult staff realized what had happened to Sam, on the inside. Apparently, when the residents were eventually yelling out the door at the staff about Sam, the staff thought it was about the deer, and so they were yelling back, "Fire department is on their way!" And the residents thought that the staff had heard their yells about Sam and that the staff was answering them about help being on the way for him. What are the odds, I thought, when I heard that?

Dennis made it through his escapade unscathed, agreeing to return indoors only after someone swiped their ungloved hand over mirrors and plate. And all I could think as they "one, two, three" d Sam onto the gurney was that it was a good thing he was unconscious for most of the commotion, because he most likely would have been telling us to save the doe first, and lord knows who there might have listened to him.

As the wheels under Sam rumbled over the back-door threshold, targeting the wide-open ambulance awaiting him, "Just slip out the back, Jack," I said aloud to no one.

* * *

That feeling of relief that Sam was alive did not last long. As I returned to the scene, where Sam's stomach contents were then being swirled by a mop, I could feel that ephemeral respite drain from my body, turning tingling to numbness, as I contemplated what I knew all too well about men in Sam's age group who have heart attacks. The odor from the vomit kept people away, which was a good thing for me, right then, so I stayed there. I knew I was going to be facing comments, compliments, "attagirl" s—for my performance. Normally, I would have enjoyed such acknowledgements, but I was too worried about Sam to enjoy anything.

Lynden, keeping to within a safe nasal distance at the community room entrance, shouted out to both me and the about-to-hurl mop swirler (former log roller), as if I or he cared, that the doe was on land and doing well. One of the four firepersons, who originally came for the doe-save, had stayed behind with a ladder. The long ladder straddled one side of the hole, reaching solid ice on both sides. From shore, the firefighter managed to lasso the doe's neck and guide her to the ladder at the edge of the hole, providing her hooves something to latch on to. The frightened animal apparently fought the pull of the rope at first, but ultimately acquiesced and followed lead, either because she caught on that she was heading towards solid ground or more likely because she had no fight left. The firewoman had been chosen to hang back for doe duty because she had rodeo experience.

As I contemplated that rescue, rubbing my arms that were still quivering from the catch of Sam, I managed to think that it was a stroke of luck for that doe that their "lake" was really a pond.

* * *

Seeking rest, I pulled a chair over to one of the tables that was holding up those seedlings and gazed through the window as the rescue activity died down, the doe having taken off, the lasso lady basking in her glory. I didn't know Sam had a heart problem. Maybe he hadn't known either. *He will now*, I thought, *if he even lives to learn about it.*

Looking down at the seedlings, myself as spent as that doe, I wondered whether, in any plant sort of way, these sprouts had sensed unrest in their environment during the chaos. Odd to think, I pondered, that Sam and I were peaceably exchanging colorless, odorless gas compounds with these plantlets one moment and yet, when these same auras began colliding traumatically, these little shoots who we cared for daily would not even be aware at some vegetal level that their supportive environment was experiencing mayhem. Did they continue using our exhaled carbon dioxide and the sun that kept shining through those windows on all of us plants and animals, to photosynthesize, during our distress? Or did they pause their growing, for even a nanosecond, in some dimension of detecting an alteration? At that moment I needed to think they sensed, somehow, someway, something.

My eyes moved from the plants to the quieted scene outside. Left on the scene now was only the maintenance man who stood with his arms folded, sadly surveying the ruts that would need repair, and all that was left of that poor creature's trauma were the tracks left by man intervening with nature in the snow that covered more than signs. My shifting thoughts then found the deer. How traumatic for that doe to be walking on what she probably thought was land one moment, almost drowning the next, no one to help her at first, and then scared to near death by the very animals who came to her rescue. Did she not know she was walking on water? Was she going for a drink? Why didn't she just eat snow?

And then, like running into a pole, it came to me, all too late. *Oh, no! Oh, how could I not have known? Sam, I am so sorry. I knew. I should have put this together. Why didn't I?* There was only one explanation, one god-damn oh-so-obvious explanation for not doing so—Donna's theory of singular focus. I was so damn focused on that deer that I never saw this coming. *I never even looked up at you, Sam, where I would have seen warning signs. Oh, my poor Sam, that doe was your Birch!*

Had I been aware, sensitive, I lamented, I could have directed Sam away from the window as soon as Lynden called out about the deer. I could have talked to Sam, soothed him, helped him through his PTSD. Shit, a younger me would never have even suggested that walk to where Sam's nightly pain gained its strength. As a nurse, I knew how to do all of that. As a younger nurse, I had done that. But as an old was-a-nurse, I could not. I could not because I did not even make the connection, the connection I had been able to make for so many people in my career, people I didn't even know, people I didn't even love.

And as with every time I contemplated my aging, I turned to thoughts of my mother. I recalled once when Mom made a comment about how hard it was for children of divorced parents to have to split their time between two homes, how it must take its toll on their developing psyches. She made that comment in front of Bonnie's recently divorced friend who had two kids who were doing just that. And Bonnie had *just* told my mother, just minutes before, warning her, about this recent divorce of her friend, her friend who my mother knew and liked quite well. "Why did she do that?" Bonnie asked me after the comment bomb. And my answer, then, was that gramma lacked sensitivity, that she did not worry or care as much about other people's feelings, now that she was older. But then on that day of the deer and my dear Sam, I could see that it was not about Mom not caring as much. It was about Mom not making the connection—the connection she would have made when she was younger and able to juggle more than one focus.

Even more worrisome to me on that day was that it occurred to me that Mom was certainly not aware that this was happening to her. And so, I pondered, is it possible that neither am I? That is, how many people, I wondered, had I been hurting that I didn't know about? Sam was one hurt that I eventually caught. *Maybe by next year*, I thought, *would I be at the point where I would never make connections and even after the fact never catch the miss, as I did with Sam?* This was, and still is, the biggest fear I have about aging—becoming out of touch with the pain and joy of others. Oh, I don't mind not getting a joke or botching a schedule, but to miss the human dynamics, the subtleties that touch the hearts of those around me, able only to pull out a thread here or there from their intricately connected webs of spirit, oblivious to their wholeness—now that is loss. It was anticipatory loss that I felt that afternoon in that still-smelling-of-Sam room, a loss which I had been able to feel before my ability to catch the connections would be replaced by unawareness, a loss that I would no longer feel when it really did happen to me, a loss that would be interpreted by others as me not caring anymore.

And to think, I sheepishly reflected, that only minutes earlier I was expecting a plant to have an ability to connect—a plant.

Once again, I could not stop crying, my sobs serving as faux air freshener to the residents who decided to stomach the stench and come to my aid. They thought I was crying because Sam was sick. They thought I was crying because I would miss him. They did not know I was crying because I *had* missed *him*, for a deer.

* * *

Later that day, stretched out in my bed, I stared at a ceiling that sported nothing worth counting. Sheep were always a bust, so I didn't even give that a try. I never had an opportunity to worry whether Jeff would live through his heart attack, so this was new territory for me. My mind was a pinball machine, bouncing off scary thoughts, ricocheting back into better thoughts that would not hold.

I felt my heart racing. Bounding pulsations in my ears signaled a blood pressure that likely measured in the vicinity of stroke land. My head felt full and sore. The memory of all four of my parents and grandparents "stroking," two very close to my age, loomed. I took an extra dose of my combination beta blocker/diuretic blood pressure pill. Though I had never done that, I felt desperate to calm my wrestling heart which was registering 120 BPM on my Fitbit. My usual resting pulse was 60, and I *was* resting. I turned on the bathroom light and closed the door within a crack of being shut, certain I would be waking several times during the night thanks to that diuretic that accompanied the beta blocker.

About half an hour later, when I was making progress with a pulse of 80, a quiet knock on the door revved up my sympathetic nervous system once again, and I felt like I was in Jamaica listening to a miniature steel drum band that was performing in my head. At the door, I recall considering whether my pulse had been loud enough to have alerted the staff to check on me, and as I then chuckled at that ridiculous thought, I slowly opened the door still half-expecting a crash cart.

Behind that door stood the person I least expected or wanted to see. Like an electric cattle prod in a cow's behind, the sight of her rendered my pulse uncountable. She was raw-faced—all make-up removed. I could not decide at that moment whether she was scarier with or without make-up. Her hair was wrapped in sponge curlers and covered in a mesh net. Her paisley polyester nightie was ankle-length and two sizes too small. And the bunny slippers complicated the whole image for me.

"B-Sylvia?" She looked at me like she caught the "B" slip. Like she was aware of her nickname and was hurt.

A deep sigh erased her wounded facial expression and then she said, "I couldn't sleep thinking about you…and Sam. I took a chance you couldn't either." Her tone was as soothing to my sprinting heart as a handful of beta blockers. My quivering lips and tear-filled eyes invited her inside, and we met for a synchronized, magnetic hug. She hugged hard, and long. I hugged hard back and waited for her to be the one to end the best hug I ever had. *Was this really happening? Was I hugging the Bingo Bitch?*

Once we were finally apart, we moved to the side of my bed where she touched my knee and said, "I know." Her words, her tone, and her touch precipitated my transition from the shock of realizing who was sitting on my bed, next to me, to sobbing into her buxomy chest.

"Can we say a prayer together, Joni?" It was a strange tone— very matter of fact yet comforting.

I nodded, shaking tears and wiping snot onto her nightgown that faintly smelled like Ciara, Mom's scent. I lamented that I never before got close enough to this woman to enjoy my mother's scent.

She reached for my hand and began to recite the "Our Father." I joined her in the "Amen." It was then that I noticed the crucifix that peeked between two buttons of her snug nightie, having managed to escape from her cavernous cleavage during our prayer. We sat quietly for a full minute after our prayer, me totally clueless as to how to proceed and she impossible to read.

Hostess. Be a hostess. "Sylvia, can I get you a cold herbal tea drink—no caffeine?"

She accepted my offer and we moved to the chairs, sipping and chatting. We started talking about the doe and Sam and Dennis collage of events. She had little sympathy for the doe and Dennis. During the conversation, I was distracted by wanting to know what caused her to search me out on that night. What loss had she suffered, I wondered, that led her to this uncharacteristic act of compassion?

Awkwardly, I asked: "Sylvia, what made you come to me in my hour of darkness?" *Lame, I thought. So very lame. I used to be so much better at this kind of thing.*

Like she was thinking *I thought you would never ask,* she jumped right in with the story of her husband's death.

Hmm. Maybe not so lame. Maybe I still had it, at least some of it.

She was clearly ready to tell her story. Correction: she appeared to *need* to tell her story.

They were married thirty years, with three grown children, when a knock on their door changed their lives forever. Behind that door stood the man who would inform Sylvia of the shocking news that she was married to a high-ranking officer in the SS; she was married to a Nazi. During his short visit, the US government representative informed them that an interrogation to determine whether Axel was the man the Polish government was looking for would begin the next day; a car would pick Axel up at 0800 hours. There was a warrant for his arrest. After a positive identification, he would be extradited to Poland where he would stand trial for war crimes.

Sylvia said that when the man stated Axel's full name, including "SS," Axel interrupted, stating he was only in the SS for six months. Axel added, in the hopes of softening the G man, that he was recruited as a Hitler Youth and that he was forced to remain a Nazi if he wanted to keep his family alive. Sylvia recalled chiming in, with a shaky voice, telling the man that her Axel was the kindest man she had ever met and that he had been an active community volunteer for all the years they were married. The man responded by explaining that he was only there to deliver the message and arrange for transport. He warned Axel to stay put, that he was being watched.

Sylvia said the man *did* soften at the end of his visit and acted like he understood the sad circumstances. He suggested Axel write down as many facts as he could remember and to contact as many witnesses as he could, while still in the US. He left offering good luck to the couple, shaking Axel's hand and bowing to Sylvia. Sylvia ended her recall of that scene with, "It wasn't his fault. He was just doing his job."

When he left, Sylvia asked Axel if he was a murderer. Axel answered that he was doing his job, as a soldier. She said she rephrased that question and asked if he killed people while in the line of duty as a soldier. He nodded yes. Needing a number, she persevered: Hundreds? He did not respond. Thousands? Tears rolled down his cheeks when he sobbed out a yes.

Sylvia found Axel dead in their bed the next morning—a heart attack after ingesting a handful of sleeping pills. Sylvia said Axel always had a hard time sleeping, and that after that visit, she finally understood why.

"I should have been suspicious," she sadly acknowledged, "because he claimed he had no family—that his mother died from cancer when he was a young child, his father died from a heart attack during the war, and that he was an only child. So now, she explained, she remains wondering whether any of that was true. And is there a whole family in Germany—grandparents, aunts, uncles, cousins—who are related to my children?" None of them were interested in finding out and neither was she.

The day of his death, the camper they had ordered was delivered—they had planned to spend their retirement years visiting their children in three different states and seeing the country. I could not resist mentally tossing a shot at the "Father" she had prayed to just minutes earlier. *What cruel timing.*

Their three children came home when they learned of their father's death. Sylvia said she did not tell them the whole truth until they were all together—that she could not bear the thought of telling that horror three separate times. That, and the wonder of whether they would even come once they learned the truth about their father, helped her decide to hold off on the disclosure.

Their son refused to attend the funeral—"middle child with a chip," Sylvia flippantly assessed. Their daughters attended the funeral, flanking their mother throughout the long day until it came time for family to approach the casket for their final goodbye. "They left me to go it alone for that. I guess I could understand—I wasn't too thrilled about saying a final goodbye to a man who betrayed me."

When Sylvia noticed my eyes welled with tears, she said, with a hint of sarcasm, "Did you know people can run out of tears?" I was stunned by the question and retorted a quick, "No." She went on to say that she had cried for a week straight after Axel's death and then she could never cry again—not when her grandson died in a car accident, not when her daughter had a miscarriage, not even on their anniversary or Axel's birthday. She claimed that nothing really mattered much after all that emotional trauma. She then talked about her anger—at Axel for not telling her; maybe they could have hidden out together if she could ever get over being married to a murderer and a liar. She was also angry at the war, at Hitler, and the Nazis. And most of all, she was angry at God for all of the above. She wondered if the anger would ever leave her. She wondered if she was being punished for something she did.

"But Sylvia, you cared enough to visit me tonight and even pray with me."

"Yes. Well, that is because I had a debt to pay. The day my husband died, before my children arrived, a neighbor who I barely knew came by for a visit. Her name was Claudia, and I didn't even know her last name then and still don't. She held me and prayed the "Our Father" with me, just like I did with you. She helped me get through that day, that day during which I seriously contemplated suicide, and I told myself then and there that I would pay back that kindness to someone, someday. And I keep my promises; I pay my debts. And this is someday."

"So, why me? Surely someone else needed your comfort in all these years."

"Because I heard you found your husband dead in bed like I did, and I like Sam. He reminds me of my Axel—well, the Axel *I* knew. He does not resemble Sam physically, but his quiet soft manner reminds me of Axel. And I'm getting old, and I don't have much time left to stand good by my promise."

So, I was an invoice on which she could stamp a comforting "paid in full." Oddly, I was okay with that.

Sylvia also talked about her impatience with people who complained about unimportant things. "So many people," she said, "just don't know what big problems are, so they make a big deal out of small potatoes. Like what is on TV or missing a bingo call on a twenty-five-cent game. I want to say to them, 'Hey, when you find out your husband is a mass murderer on one day and you bury him the next, then you can whine to me about a twenty-five-cent bingo game.' But what good would it do? They are just pissy pots—every one of them."

It was amazing to watch her transform from the new soft Sylvia to the ole Sylvia in just a few short minutes. Then, once solidly back to her Bingo Bitch persona, she checked her watch, abruptly rose, and announced, "It's after midnight. What in the hell are we doing staying up this late? She then walked out of my room without a goodbye or a wave.

Whirl winded by the extremes of emotions I had just experienced—comforted, comforter, stepped over—I attempted to collect myself. I wondered if she had shared her story with anyone else at Borealis. I had been tempted to ask, but she left before I got the chance. My guess was that she had not. I could not even begin to imagine the sense of betrayal she had experienced and likely still was experiencing—it explained so much. I noticed she did not wear a wedding ring as so many other widows did at Borealis, as I did. Suddenly I saw her toughness, her bitchiness, for what it was—fighting back, preserving self, releasing stored-up anger. After our visit, I was not sure if I liked her any better; I was not even sure which Sylvia I preferred. But I *did* know that I loved her. I was left, however, with having to deal with the realization that the nurse in me should have sought *her* out, should have recognized her behavior as the sign of a bruised soul needing comfort, needing a nurse. Another person I had missed—*and counting.*

* * *

The next day, the staff and residents were buzzing about the deer and about their dearest resident, for Sam had a way with the Borealis clan. It was anxiety-producing for me to listen to them when I didn't know if he was alive and well, dying, or dead. This was certainly not in the spirit of the HIPAA law, I churned, for there I was, unable to hear one damn word about Sam's condition, about a person I loved as much as anyone I had loved in my life, and someone I believed loved me. Just one more example, I thought, of a law being created as a quick and easy fix for problems that originated from lack of discretion and judgment in all those health-care workers who should have known better in the first place. And because this bad professional judgment had hurt patients, a law was made to answer that problem and to hell with the people whom *that* law would hurt.

I had to find out about Sam's condition. Finally, I came up with the idea that I could ask the staff to call Tammy and ask her to call me. My mistake was asking someone on the day shift. They, who spend too much of their time in meetings about laws and regulations and little about people, were not willing to call a resident's daughter for another resident, especially when the resident had "age-associated memory impairment" for nice, mild dementia for real—their real, that is, not mine. Not good for business, I took a wild guess.

Foiled, but desperate, I approached someone on the evening shift. I picked the most naive-appearing staffer of the three and told her I just remembered that, on his way out the door, Sam had told me something important about his house that he wanted me to tell his daughter. She suggested I tell her and that she would tell Tammy. I was prepared for that. I told her that he expressly told me not to tell anyone but Tammy. Her eyes rolled slightly but she bought it, poor thing. She called Tammy right in front of me, and I heard Tammy say, "Put her on if she's there." I oddly hadn't thought through the plan that far, but I managed to ask the staffer to give me a private moment to tell Tammy the secret message, and, poor thing, again, she complied, leaving Sam's folder wide open for me to sneak a peek. I didn't. But I finally understood that she and others like her were the *why* behind the HIPAA law. Alas, I thought, they were out there, and so maybe there was indeed a need for that law. Except that law surely did not stop *her*.

I fessed up to Tammy about just wanting a report on Sam. She understood. Sam was alive. He had a small inferior MI, she said, like she wasn't very familiar with the terminology. But I was, and that was good news. *So, why didn't he call?* I wondered. "Tammy, is he awake?"

"Oh, yes. Very awake, but not very with it. I just gave permission to sedate him at night. His days and nights are all mixed-up, the doctor said, and so his behavior is as unpredictable throughout the day as it has been at night. He has a sitter, they call it, around the clock. He has pulled out his tubes and tried to crawl over the bedrails." The image of that scene was crystal clear in my mind, for I knew that side of Sam all too well, not to mention a plethora of my former patients who had fit that description.

"Tammy, does he have a history of heart problems?" I asked, knowing I was again giving away that we were not as close as perhaps she had thought, as perhaps I had thought.

"No. Well, I don't think so. I guess I assumed he didn't because he never mentioned that he did, though he is a very private person. But the doctor never mentioned any history, either, and I never thought to ask. I guess I assumed this was all new."

My hands were quaking like aspens in breeze, causing me to drop the phone under the desk, out of reach. *If only I could kneel.* I began yelling at the phone for Tammy to not hang up when the staffer barged in, having heard the ruckus. She picked up the phone and looked at me like I was who I had been pretending to be at Borealis, and I was never so disappointed in one of my accomplishments as I was at that moment.

She told Tammy, "I'm sorry, I probably should not have let her call you."

I could not hear what Tammy said because the staffer had deliberately walked away from me while Tammy was speaking. And then she said the most beautiful words I had heard since before Jeff died. She said, as she grabbed for a sticky note and handed it to me along with a pen, "She wants your phone number. She will call you tomorrow with an update."

No wonder, I thought, that Sam wanted so much to protect this fruit of his, who relievedly had not fallen far from her magnificent father tree.

* * *

The next morning, I was in the midst of leaving Andy a phone message to arrange for him to take me on a field trip to visit Sam in the hospital when my phone alerted me that there was an incoming call. I abandoned Andy's message mid-sentence, which would only serve to add to my subterfuge, although that was the furthest thing from my mind at the time. It was Tammy. Sam was doing better, no more delirium, discharge was planned for a day or two, and he would be going home with Tammy for as long as it took for a full recovery. "Or forever, if I have my way," she closed.

Forever, if she had her way. Tammy lived an hour from Borealis and hours away from my home. I could not decide, in that moment, if that would be good or bad . . . for us. I had enough of a time deciding if there even *was* an us. Nor would I be able to decide those same ifs during all the lonely days and nights that followed. And while there was definitely an "us" in my mind, I was certainly not sure whether there was one in his. I had never experienced this type of uncertainty—Jeff and I fell in love as virtual children, early twenties. We descended together like a duet parachute drop, no time for either of us to even consider who "us" was, especially when neither of us had yet spent much time considering who ourselves were. This feeling of uncertainty was more new territory.

Sam began calling every day, but his calls were limited to idle chit-chat. He sounded good, but distant. I missed so much about him; I missed so much about me with him. I found it difficult to concentrate on my project, and when one gets to these advancing years, the concern is always that any form of inability may not be transient. I lost interest in the residents at Borealis. I lost interest in myself, struggling to manage a daily shower, missing too often without shame, and I gave up on my hair completely. I was losing weight that others could notice—I just was not hungry. I didn't even bother to weigh myself for a gratifying Petunia Pig entry.

It had come upon just over a month left of my contract with Borealis. I could extend the contract, but I had no desire to do so. I wasn't even sure about writing this book.

And then Sam invited me to Tammy's home for dinner. He would pick me up! Everything changed with that call, and I felt like I was going to the ultimate *senior* prom, only with a chaperone half my age. I decided that if we got a chance to talk alone, I would have to tell Sam that I was leaving Borealis and why. I would have to tell him. I would have to tell him. I would have to tell him. I would have to tell him.

Oh God, I don't want to tell him.

I waited for Sam in the reception area, near the front desk. I got there almost an hour early so I was sure to be able to come out to him in the parking lot, sparing him possible staff and resident interrogation. I must admit that I was anxious about what to wear, intimidated by the father-daughter duo who dressed to the nines. I chose my short grey linen blazer, a black tailored-fit dress shirt, and black gabardine slacks. It wasn't very springy, but it was all I had at Borealis that wasn't comfy casual. It had been so long that I felt like I was playing dress-up.

As I sat on the loveseat facing the front "campus," I noticed a pair of mergansers doing their best to swim on the north edge of the pond, the only open water. One ducked down, probably for a fish—the pond was stocked with panfish for the residents, staff, and visitors who liked to angle. Borealis-bound residents would line the dining room windows to watch the children on weekends, waiting to hear "Got one" through the one and only window that could be opened at Borealis. But it was too early for fishing that spring—ice was technically not completely out owing to a menopausal mother nature with hot and cold flashes who sent our little pond into a solid versus liquid identity crisis for nearly a month. But no one told the birds.

One of the residents, Helen, who was also waiting for a ride, commented about the mergansers, "They look like they are drowning, but they are just fishing, right?" I smiled and answered a colloquial "Yep." The saving of the doe was evidently still on Helen's mind. It seemed peculiar to me that anyone who lived in and among these lands of lakes would not know that about ducks, but then again, I was recently observed not knowing that Christmas was not in June.

"It's not even fishing season, is it?" I left that one alone.

Like they are drowning . . . Like they are drowning. Helen's words stuck in my grey matter like an annoying jingle. I looked at the pond, massaging my temples to rub out the neuronal glitch. There was a short floating fishing dock that jutted out from its south end that caught my eye. In that spring, before ice out, that dock, covered in terraced snow blown high from the north wind, looked a lot like something was jutting out from under the water, at about a thirty-degree angle. I got up, trance-like, and walked to the community room to eye the dock from those windows. From that angle, the dock appeared to be even more elevated above the surface.

Could it be? Oh, God, could it be? Could Sam's PTSD episodes be triggered by this pond?

He always wanted to get out through the front door. Was he trying to save Birch, every night, over and over again? Was that why his episodes were so much worse at Borealis? And why didn't I see this earlier? Certainly, I should have recognized the pond as a trigger during the doe incident, if not well before then. I imagine that anyone reading this has been yelling at me, since my first mention of Sam's episodes, "The pond, duh!"

The thought of Sam going through the worst day of his life over and over, night after night, made me angry. With whom, though, I wondered, was I angry? I didn't know, but my racing heart and my flushed face made me feel like I had enough strength and energy to take down a Sumo. But no one to wrestle, except Helen, and that just wouldn't be right, so I chose God. And I started crying and then worrying about Sam seeing me all cried out.

God, how could you be so cruel? Even Hitler could not come up with this measure of torture! But then again, you created him. Speaking of torture, and as long as I am already knee-deep in this, I would like to get something off my mind that has been bothering me since I was a child: Why did your son have to be tortured and die to save us? You are God—couldn't you figure out another way? And we know the man on that cross wasn't totally on board with his sacrificial lamb role—that "why have you forsaken me?" line tells us that. Not that I am calling you a bad dad, but it just does not square with my image of a loving father. Okay, now I am up to my eyeballs. Understand, please, that I am feeling like Sam landed in your net and you threw him back, and then you never even noticed that I was in that net with him. So isn't it understandable that I can relate to that forsaking sentiment? And I wonder if you care about that. I have spent a lifetime counting on the fact that you did, but that belief has been tragically tested over and over in my life, and I am worried that this test may just be the straw. I am also somewhat worried about expressing all of this to you, but when I consider that you already know what I am thinking, I figure: what difference does it make? I didn't hear you say: Right?

Jeff, I sure hope heaven is a stress-free zone, because if not, I am certain you must be flipping out right about now, and I am sorry but....

Helen snapped me out of yet another one-sided celestial conversation, noticing my sniveling and asking, "Are you okay, honey?"

What to say? And as I looked over at sweet Helen, who was forever waiting for someone, I figured what would she know if she didn't know that ducks duck? I weakly appeased, "Thanks, Helen. I had something in my eye, but I got it out."

* * *

Sam looked better than ever, rested, and relaxed, and for the first time ever, for my eyes, he wore jeans! We both smiled the same hoodwinked smile when we saw one another, each of us having tried to make the other comfortable by matching our respective styles, trading places in the process. *What next?* I thought. *Tammy in grey sweats?* Neither of us uttered a word about the paradox, and that was what I loved about our relationship—we didn't have to.

He didn't seem to notice that I had been crying, and if he did, the something in my eye fib was ready to roll off my tongue. I wanted to tell him about what I discovered that might be causing his night terrors, but only when the time was right, I decided, and that would probably be when he returned to Borealis, if he ever did. I wondered if my decision to wait had anything to do with my fear of him not returning coupled perhaps with not wanting to give him another reason to not return, but, I resolved, in the reception area with Helen, to pull a Scarlett O'Hara and think about that tomorrow.

We pulled up to a tidy bright white Cape Cod, topped with cedar shingles and showcasing two dormers positioned like quotation marks punctuating a front door that shouted "Welcome." Forest green shutters flanked the multipaned windows that were way too clean for early spring in the north country. A recently planted shelterbelt of cedars, which would one day say no to the north winds that gain speed over adjacent farmland, smacked heavily of Sam in its design. The well-manicured vacant flowerpots and beds read like a marquis announcing up and coming shows. And the landscaping—oh, the landscaping—was of the nature that causes the death of many a squirrel as road-bound necks turn into rubber for a glance. Thankfully for the squirrels, the long and winding drive precluded a solid view of the house from the road. Intimidating.

As would someone who played a significant role in the development of this scene, I felt Sam surveying my face for a reaction. "Beautiful home," I managed. I wanted to say something that suggested I had an eye for domain detail, but I would have needed a thesaurus. Sam strutted aside me, tickling my nose with his multicolored fanned feathers, the proud papa that he was.

I expected an *In-A-Gadda-Da-Vida*-length doorbell, but, surprise, it was just a ding-donger. Tammy's smile was so energized, it met me even before she opened the door. She wore simply a sweater and slacks, although the sweater was probably cashmere. I was so glad I had rejected my bibs.

"Joni, welcome." With a cheek kiss, she said to Sam, "Dad." He had been *living* there, and he still got a hello kiss after having been gone less than two hours. Apparently, the turn-around interval for welcoming her dad with a kiss was somewhere in the range of a loving dog's. *Wow*, I envied.

The inside of Tammy's home was sterile modern and artsy, with clear glass kitchen cabinets that answered my decades-long question about who would want their kitchen stuff showing. Sam was unusually chatty and even playful with me in front of Tammy. I fought the wonder of whether he was playful with Jane, largely because I knew that was a slippery slope that was not likely to be gracefully navigated by one who had been uncontrollably crying less than an hour ago.

Sam had made dinner, lasagna, apparently not unusual for him, I gleaned, from their discourse and from watching him move about the kitchen like he had merely rewound a well-played tape. A man looking like he belonged in a kitchen seemed so odd to me, considering my father only entered our kitchen to eat, and Jeff's one and only attempt at cooking began and ended with egg salad that started with scrambled eggs. After major razzing, Jeff self-limited to coffee, sandwiches, and anything that came fully prepared from a can or the freezer. He said his mother was to blame, having been a terrible cook. His sister, conversely, talked of their dear departed mother like she was Carmelita Pope—funny how that works.

Sam's grandchildren were loudly absent at that gathering, "off to friends for the weekend." Tammy's husband was in China on business, "pimping for investments to research an environmentally friendly replacement for plastic." Their absence caused me to wonder if I was there for Sam and Tammy to tell me something bigger than I had to tell them. But there went my rabbit mind again, ahead of the tortoise but not likely to win the race. Why couldn't I just accept that maybe this was the perfect time for them to have me over because otherwise they would likely be bored as just the two of them on a Saturday evening?

The dinner and conversation went smoothly, like we all three had known each other for much longer than a few months. In fact, I felt even more comfortable with Sam and Tammy than I did with my own family ever since I had taken on my Borealis-Joni role with them, in some ways, even before. I only had to be my real self with Tammy and Sam, and that was a surprising relief that left me anxious to abandon my work and get back to what was left of the old me.

Sam was an excellent cook. I had always thought that lasagna just tasted like spaghetti and meatballs except with wide flat spaghetti and crumbly meatballs. But Sam's lasagna had its own special amazing flavor that I could not quite place, and which he refused to share. "We—I've been trying to get him to give me that recipe for years," Tammy said, catching herself on the "we" that once went with their family.

As the evening progressed, I could not keep my eyes off Tammy because of the way she looked at Sam. She adored her father, and she read his every nonverbal cue. If he glanced in the direction of green, she asked, "More salad, Dad?" When he squinted ever so slightly, she got up immediately and adjusted the shade. And when he spoke, she leaned her chin on her folded hands and just took him in with eyes that deserved the reflection of a newborn's baby blues. I thought about how my children usually didn't even look at me when I spoke, and I wondered what I did or didn't do to not warrant such revering. But, I decided, it probably wasn't a do, or not do, phenomenon. It probably instead had to do with who he was, and who I wasn't— there goes that question again—for he was a parent who probably wouldn't lie to his children, and I wasn't.

Tammy left us alone after our spumoni ice cream dessert, claiming a need to make some phone calls. And there could not have been a better time to tell Sam about my project, but I couldn't do it.

Not there. Not then. He was so happy and at ease, I just could not drive a stake through that. I thought about how he might even be relieved that, like him, I didn't really need to be at Borealis, but ever since he told me that I had a lot of class for not allowing Tammy to tell me about Birch, I had the feeling my deception was going to change things between us. And would he think he would be in my book, with or without his permission, as in, I had used him?

My world of deceit was closing in on me, from all angles. I had been shrinking from telling my children, also, melting like the Wicked Witch of the West. And furthermore, I was willing to bet I could have effortlessly slipped into her black curled toe shoes with a perfect rendition of "I'll get you, my pretty..." on my lying Noni lips.

In fact, on one of her weekly visits, Bonnie had brought up the subject of the Borealis contract renewal, but I masterfully changed her subject. When faking dementia, changing subjects was a handy tool that I now admit I have come to miss.

Furthermore, it was no surprise that more than one of the Borealis admin staff had also approached me about reupping my contract, stressing that they "could not guarantee my room, or any room for that matter, without a signed contract, and, keep in mind that spring typically brings with it an influx of new residents." I tried to imagine what that statement would sound like if I were a resident who was in doubt about staying, perhaps hoping to change my family's mind about my mind. I wondered if they ever gave that a thought before they delivered their nippy message. I felt pressured to say something but replied only that I would have to talk with my children.

Alas, I was dodging many discussion topics with many people. But it was getting any easier. Accordingly, the long ride back to Borealis with Sam was studded with empty repartees that strung together like popcorn on a Christmas tree, leaving little room for the sine qua non of our relationship. I did manage to pull out of Sam, waiting until we were in the Borealis parking lot so as not to distract his driving, that he was still experiencing night terrors but that, as usual, away from Borealis, the episodes were less frequent and less traumatic. I wanted to bring up my theory about the Borealis lake/pond perhaps being a catalyst for the intensity of his bouts, but I did not dare take that risk right before he was facing the drive home. I have always amazed myself with my ability to rationalize—probably why I was so good at lying.

After Sam cheek-kissed me goodnight and I returned the restrained valediction, I asked when I would see him again, and he answered in vintage Sam, "Soon, Ace, if I have anything to do with it."

And that about sums up this whole aging gig for me: "If we have anything to do with it."

Just Slip Out the Back, with Jack

On a Friday, one week before the expiration of my contract, I informed Borealis that Jack Spiewak, my attorney holding DPAHC, would be picking me up the next morning to take me home and, firmly, that none of my significant others should be notified of this move. I did not want Andy and Bonnie finding out from Borealis. I made no mention of my project to Borealis, so as far as they knew, I was still gravy-drinking Joni, though I had abandoned all cover by that point. They would probably be surmising that daily cribbage was a new cure for dementia—oops, I mean AAMI.

Sam still did not know about any of this—my project, or my move. I had no reason to believe anyone from Borealis would contact him, but the anxiety attached to that remote possibility caused me to tentatively plan a visit with Sam for the day after my homecoming.

Home brought forth a flood of emotions that I did not anticipate. Jack was not the best at comforting me, lawyer that he was, especially because he joined me in not knowing what I was crying about. Maybe, I recall thinking, it was simply that the last time I had been in my home I trusted that my children loved me, and I could no longer count on that being the case when my story was told.

At my request, Jack called Andy (probably wakened him because his shop didn't open until eleven on Saturdays) and said that I was home and fine, and that when I would tell them that my mind was fine, and that it always had been, to believe me. And then Jack closed with, "Best for you and Bonnie to come here together, and plan on trying to understand." I was surprised--his sensitivity was improving. I tried to guess what my children would be thinking when they heard that portion of the news, but I was too close to the fire to see their forest for all those damn trees girdling my maternal perspective.

Jack hollowly asked if I wanted him to stay until my children arrived. "Of course not, Jack. Who knows when—shit, *if*, they will even come," I quipped, watching him spit out that hook at the sound of not. "Besides, it's Saturday—I can't afford your weekend rate." I had chosen a Saturday to avoid the brass at Borealis, to avoid stressing Bonnie on a workday, and because I knew Andy had high school helpers who could run his shop on Saturdays. Additionally, Jack was willing to give-up his Saturday morning to drive me home—well not exactly *give*.

With a half-smile and a "Good luck" on his barrister lips, like he wasn't quite sure we wouldn't both serve time or pay fines for this, Jack slipped out the back.

I had at least an hour, probably two. I needed distraction; I needed to be busy. I looked at the suitcases and boxes, appearing small in my large house compared to their expenditure of my Borealis closet. As I approached the mound and smelled Borealis, I knew this was not the distraction I needed. I heard, barely, a screeching critter sound—blue jay or squirrel, wasn't sure—and realized my right ear was partially blocked as it often was, and so I decided to irrigate my ear. Whenever my ear was blocked, I felt like I was in a bubble or like I was hearing under water. And, I thought, it just would not do to have a blocked ear, for what if I thought Bonnie said, as was typical when she left me in anger or frustration, "Whatever; call me," when what she really said was, "Never call me."

I made a mental game of coming up with other possible mishears, and most of them were seriously stretched, such as, on her way out the door "Good luck" may sound like "Get f---ed," and although Bonnie had never before said the F word in my earshot, then again I never lied to her before about anything beyond the soothing nature of "Of course Gramma loves you as much as your cousins," and then there was Santa. Come to think of it, I thought, her for-real, angry, sarcastic "Good luck" while walking out the door would probably be conveying the same message as my construed vulgar mishear, so not to worry about that distinction. *A troubled mind is a terrible thing to have to occupy.*

Clear-eared and an hour and forty-five minutes later, I heard the consecutive slams of two car doors. I wondered where they had met. I peeked out the window and saw my children walking, fingertips stuffed in the pockets of their tight pants, wide-striding towards my front door. They had pensive and driven faces, and closed mouths. Upon entry, Bonnie's tongue occupied her left cheek. I said "Hi", but they said nothing. They should have been wearing jackets. I held back. Their clothes looked like they were picked off the floor from the night before, Andy's fleece pullover full of golden hairs from his retriever who probably used it for a pillow all night. I used that uncomfortable moment to privately bemoan that I had never gotten my children to use a hamper.

Both Bonnie and Andy began rotating their necks a lot more degrees than mine ever turned, searching my home for what they probably did not know. It hurt to see them like that, but who was I to expect sympathy for any of my hurts?

Bonnie opened with a curt, "What's up, Mom?" She was pissed but restrained.

So, at that point, I spilled my guts for a good five minutes, proffering an explanation I had rehearsed and eventually ran by Jack, captivating my children's attention like only Santa ever could. Finished, I watched them thaw out, Bonnie faster than Andy, like she was in the sun and he was not.

And then came Bonnie, full throttle, delivering, give or take, three "How could you put us through this?" s, two "How could we ever trust you again?" s (usually double-teamed with "You are so selfish"), four "Seriously, who does this?" s, five "Unbelievable" s, three "Andy, can you believe this?" s, one "Sonuvabitch!" and too many "Oh my god" s and "How could you?" s to count.

All in all, I thought she took it well. Because what I did not hear was "I never want to see you again," "We are done," "Leave us alone," or any other relationship-ending statements, and she only swore once. And never did I hear "I'll sue you if you put me in your damn book," like I had expected to hear, like Jack told me to expect to hear.

Andy, however, appeared to take it much worse. He said nothing during both my explanation and Bonnie's rant. His eyes said all what Bonnie's said and more, the worst of which was that he was terribly disappointed in me. And when he left, he did not offer his usual "In a while, crocodile" to which I would respond, "Later, gator," not that I was expecting. All he said was, "I'm going to leave now," and it was not clear to me whether he was speaking to both of us, or to just Bonnie. Not "I need to go," not "I have to go." That is, no sign of his leaving being jump-started by some external source, but merely a resigned announcement of exit. *What are you saying to me, Andy?* I wondered. He was always more difficult to read than was ankle-deep messaging Bonnie. With Andy, a coast-guard-approved life jacket was required.

Oh, Andy. Oh, god, help him, them. Jeff, you too, please do whatever you can do to make this better for all of us.

When they left, less than an hour after they had arrived, it felt like it was for good. Having searched their faces, I couldn't detect any signs that indicated they might see me again, not that I knew what that would look like, but I sought evidence, nonetheless.

I had made them suffer. Now it was their turn, and to think I was the one who taught them to take turns. As I looked over at my suitcase with its secret compartment, I contemplated whether, if they were out of my life, I would ever be able to concentrate on writing, and if I didn't write about Borealis, all their pain was for nothing.

And if you could torture Sam as you did, god, I would not put it past you to do this to me.

Ever since Sam's heart attack and the dawn of my belief that the pond was behind it, it was becoming increasingly difficult to see god as my friend. I began questioning his role in my life, even his existence, and off that trajectory, I decided then and there that he no longer merited upper-case status for me, like Christ for Angie's Abe, but for different reasons. But oddly that did not stop me from talking to him, wishing he could be a *He* again for me. I worried about this fractured bond, hoped beyond hope that it was transient, and eventually decided that if god was God, he would not only be able to handle my disavowal, but also forgive me for it one day. And that, for me, has been the best thing about this relationship—an unwavering confidence, trust, which enables inner peace. For that, I am so very grateful.

I also realized on that day that Sam and I had never talked about religion. And so I wondered in which case, if any, Sam held his creator, and also in which case the two of them held me.

Feeling very lower case in all my long-term relationships, I turned my thoughts to shorter term Sam and mulled over how I would tell him. I decided to call him and invite him to lunch, "at my home, not Borealis." He took a pensive moment and replied, "Are you home for a visit?" I answered with an uncontrollable high-pitched voice, the likes of which I had forever decried was used all too often by too many women to solicit cooperation, the likes of which he had never before heard from me: "No. Home for good. I'll tell you all about it tomorrow. Noon?" I couldn't believe my ears. Valley girl. All that was missing was the gum.

He sounded unaffected by the news that I was home, asking what to bring, getting my address, ending the conversation like he did on his daily calls since he awakened as Sam after his heart attack. Again, that self-doubt swelled like dough in a warm oven, leaving me in the wonder of who in the hell I was to this man that this unforeseen information was accepted so casually, when I should have been grateful that he was not upset.

Oh, Jeff, I mean it—you must have been canonized a saint by now if god is paying attention. Not like he pays attention. To me.

The next morning, I woke at four with that feeling that tells you there is no possibility of returning to sleep. Back to the task of occupying my mind before I lost it. I decided, after my third cup of coffee and second *Andy Griffith* episode, to set out for the supermarket in my car that badly needed air in the tires because it had stayed in the same spot all winter. I didn't want to spend the effort to fill them, and as my tires began to squeal on the turn out of the driveway, feeling every piece of base gravel #3 that made its way to the surface (*I know, Jeff, this is so bad for the brakes, not to mention the tires*), I met up with a white unmarked shrunken delivery truck.

The driver lowered his window and yelled above Braid Paisley singing "Ticks": "Delivery. Car or door?"

I yelled back, "Car," because I was curious, patting the passenger seat as I caught the young man's eyes on his way out the door, reminding myself of Angie. The driver was wearing shorts on a day way too cold for shorts, but I fought and won the nagging desire to point that out to him. I seriously—scratch that—earnestly needed someone to mother.

He placed the large package, which was looking and smelling very floral, on the passenger seat off which I had hurriedly cleared of a Borealis information folder and several books I had long ago, a whole loving family ago, planned to take to the resale shop. I waited until the white stubby van was out of sight, and as I fumbled to hastily open the card, I murmured to myself, *"Please, god, let it be from my children and please not cut flowers."* I so needed to know things were right with them.

Neither of my lower-case prayers came true—*go figure*—I unwrapped cut roses from Sam. "Welcome home," the card read. Another one of those Jeff moments swept over me, this one like a mist of ammonia over mosquito-stung dermis. Another reminder that Jeff knew me, and Sam did not. Jeff would have known not to send me cut flowers—magnificent lives selfishly amputated from their energy to please my eyes and nose with their beauty and scent until a day or two later when those same eyes and that same nose would sense only their decay—reminding me of my own.

Memories of when I first started hating cuts stalled me, half-in, half-out of my driveway. My car filled with the reminiscent tang of isopropyl alcohol and tincture of benzoin layered over Christian Dior Obsession, calling back a time when I received a similar package while the over-fragranced PA was removing my surgical dressing from where my breast used to be. When she left, I plucked what I decided was half the petals from each of the vase-bound daisy specimens that were taking up too much room on my overbed table, reciting, "He'll still love me; he'll love me not." And then I fell half-asleep but awake enough to hear Jeff utter "What the heck?" to that pathetic display. And he sensitively never gave me the opportunity to do that again.

On my way to market, I managed to remember that Sam liked swiss cheese and bacon, so I decided on Quiche Lorraine, a spinach salad, and keep-me-real-busy home-made bread sticks. And just in case the baking bread did not take out the stale, closed-up house smell, I picked up some "Calm Sea" scented wax cubes." They had me at "Calm."

* * *

Twelve on the dot—no surprise—he came in wearing a baby-blue sweater over an off-white crisp collared shirt, in lockstep, thank you, Sam, with my theme of calm. And his pants, back to Dockers. Following the pleasantries and a thank you for the flowers, I opened with a line it took me all night to come up with, "Well, Sam, either we get rid of the elephant in this dining room now, or we have lunch first, but in the latter case I cannot guarantee this pachyderm will not fight us for the quiche."

Characteristically, Sam did not disappoint, extemporaneously surpassing my contrived wit, "Not to worry, Ace, they're vegetarians, but if you'd rather talk first, I'm fine with that. I might have to get ugly with him over that salad, though. That looks amazing."

I loved when he called me "Ace." I hated that he was not more serious about my mystery. Perhaps his dipstick for serious had evolved since the accident.

I looked over at the kitchen worktable and thought about all the effort I had put into that meal and then struggled with the thought of whether Sam would ever stay to eat it once we talked. But I could not wait any longer to relieve my discomfort, probably more like *share* it, if being honest.

"Sam, I'm not who you think I am." I could not make eye contact with anything but the parquet floor.

"I know." When I looked up, there was a smirk on his face that I didn't like, and which hung there amidst spots in the form of the floor's herringbone mosaic. Did he really say he knew? How could he know? Who told him? Andy and Bonnie could not have gotten to him this soon. They probably didn't even know his name or that he was someone special to me. The only others who knew about the project were Jack and Doc Chott, and they didn't know Sam. He doesn't know. He couldn't know.

"You know what?" I asked, like I was a teacher delivering an oral test to a kid who just ticked me off royally.

"That you were doing research at Borealis. Right?" He looked smug when he made the comment, which was mildly annoying, especially when I was beginning to think he was more in control of my disclosure than I was.

"How long have you known?" Now I was down to just plain curious.

"Ever since the first time you beat me at cribbage," he winked, presumably an attempt to let me know that he was joking, but he had me, with or without the wink, for I did not yet catch his humor. Watching the ball go over my head, he quickly added, "No, seriously, I spent a lot of time with you. I figured it out."

"Figured it out? Like how did you figure it out?" I asked, a little ruffled about my inability to fool Sam like I thought I had easily fooled others.

He came behind me and rubbed my shoulders. "Let's see . . . You had no physical reason to be there. In fact, I caught some pretty slick moves you made when you thought no one was watching. You visited with different residents almost every day. And hmm," he paused, and then went on, "seriously now, you *could* beat me at cribbage, so I knew that mind of yours was working. What else? Oh, you are a nurse with advanced degrees. And, you went to your room early every night, you slept late, which means you went to sleep late, yet you didn't know about one damn show on TV. Joni, I kept score and did the math."

I felt my face flush. I felt foolish realizing that he had known for so long. "Why didn't you say something, Sam?"

"Why would I? You were doing well, it seemed. We were doing well. And I wasn't one hundred percent sure until you called yesterday."

"And it didn't bother you that I was deceiving you?" I asked, suddenly feeling angry about worrying so much about how to tell him, and back to not knowing at whom to direct my anger. And then there was this: what kind of person is not upset if someone they love is lying to them?

"You didn't deceive me, Joni. Well, not directly. You never told me you had dementia. When I asked why you were at Borealis, you never answered me. That, by the way, was my strongest clue."

He was right. I had not lied to him outright, but I was not forthcoming. But being not forthcoming did not sound nearly as bad as being a liar. I liked that assessment.

I turned and reigned him in for a hug that was quiche-scorching in length. I cried harder than I cried when Jeff died because, I later decided, I had not been dealing with guilt over Jeff's death. I sobbed about Andy and Bonnie, and Sam said nothing, just held me, tightly, and stroked my head.

Sam and I were good. I had somebody to love, and to love me, for sure.

Thank you, Jeff, and by the way, you make a great extraterrestrial husband. And give a nod to your friend up there, for me.

* * *

Sam returned to Borealis a few days later, against Tammy's will, and I still hadn't heard from Andy or Bonnie. My plan with the grandkids was to wait for the weekend and then try. But before I tried, Bonnie's oldest called. Apparently, she was the only one of the children Bonnie had told, and she called just to say she loved me even if I had lied. I told my eleven-year-old-going-on-fifty granddaughter that everything would be okay soon, that we just needed to give her mom and uncle Andy some more time. If only her mother could catch up to her, developmentally, I daydreamed. She also said that her daddy wasn't mad at me, and I spared her the reason for that being that he and I were never close enough for my betrayal to matter to him.

As far as Andy's children were concerned, he had married even older than Bonnie had, and his children were too young to be told any of what I had done. His wife? She would go with this where Andy went—he wisely was her compass.

I visited Sam the day after his return to Borealis. I had not slept the night before, awake with palpitations that began to sound to me like the message I wanted to deliver to him, in code: "I-t-s t-h-e-p-o-n-d-s-a-m."

We decided we just *had* to meet outside for it was an unseasonably warm spring day, the kind of day we Northerners claim we'll have to pay for later, because the mother of Northwoods nature rules with a heavy hand, teaching us the hard stormy lessons, grounding us all too often within a moment's notice, doling out her motherly warmth sparingly, oh so sparingly most springs, most years. And so, when we awaken to such a rare vernal morn in these lands north of the fortieth latitude, this matriarch is treated by us, her children, like the biblical father treated his prodigal son, with such intense appreciation for her unexpected expression of comfort as would come from any offspring who finds their mother's affection only once in their while. It is what the people in the sunshine lands miss, I do believe— that "you *do* love me" moment towards their mother of nature that makes such a day so very important to us.

We stopped at the bench overlooking the water, a bench that only two weeks ago warded off potential warmers with its thick layer of crusty snow and pock-studded ice. As we sat, Sam looked down at my feet and noticed an early scrawny dandelion sprouting from each of my toe shoes. "She who walks with the flowers," he said, casting his arm around me and squeezing out the laugh that was on its way out of my lungs. I loved that he called dandelions flowers, named such by so few, past kindergarten. We sat in silence for as long as it took a merganser to swim around that pond at least the square root of twenty-five times. Yes, there I was, counting and wishing I could have been in that moment with Sam, but instead I was distracted by wanting to use this time to talk with Sam about my pond theory.

"Let's walk the shoreline, Sam." I was still not ready.

When we came to the short dock, I took off my shoes while visions of my bare feet meeting dock danced in the part of my brain that stored my youth. Stepping on the weathered planks, I flashed back to my child of six, running across my grandfather's dock to chase what I called a frog, and my father called a toad. And then the stab of pain! Forevermore, as a child, the pain of the dreaded sliver loomed with every barefoot step I took over rough wood surfaces.

But as an old person, I mused, the dread now became the *absence* of that pain when that same sliver would touch nerves that were too worn to speak up. The body surely likes to play games with the mind, or is it the other way around?

Sam chose to shed no footwear and instead to sit crisscross applesauce against the post nearest me. We sat again in silence for nearly a half hour, except for the noisy waterfowl and crows, which was possible for me to do only because I was rehearsing how I was going to have this very personal conversation with him, on that day, near that pond. He knew something was up. I could tell. I appreciated that he did not rush me.

When my toes were nearly blue, we made our way back to the bench, me barefoot, Sam with his arm around me, giving the home crew something worth window-watching in their boring-all-of-us lives.

We snapped together on that bench like jigsaw puzzle pieces finding each other. Feeling Sam along the length of my right side, I fought the urge to blurt, knowing it would lead to rambling, accelerated speech, and an end to the moment. I kept my eyes fixed on the pond, hoping he would join me. We were in direct line with the dining room window and so with my eyes peeled on the pond I whispered, "What do you see, Sam?"

He pulled away slightly, looked at me curiously, and then followed my gaze to the water, answering as a typical Wisconsonite: "A lake?" His expression did not change, and it would have been natural for him to tease me about the self-evident nature of my question, and the very fact that he did not take that opportunity suggested to me he was experiencing something related to the pond that was grabbing his attention.

I told him that I saw something sticking out of the water and then watched carefully for his reaction. He took his time searching for what I was referring to and then his right cheek began to twitch, but otherwise he seemed unaware of my lead. "Yeah, the dock. What's this all about, Ace?"

I told him. I don't even recall the exact way I told him because I was so nervous, so worried, worried especially that he would have another heart attack.

I do recall that he said that I could have something there. He rose stiffly from the bench and took a few steps toward the dock, me following, examining, looking back at the community room window from where he would have seen that dock, day after day, as he faced it not only during meals, but when we played cribbage. It was as if his subconscious had tucked away the daytime scene, and then let it go free at night.

"So, if your theory is right, Joni, what do I do about it?"

To answer that question, I took his hand and led him back to the bench to tell him my squirrel story, as I had planned.

"Sam, sit down, please. This is fairly long." He knew I was serious, so he sat down, arm over the back of the bench behind my shoulders, his eyes fixed on the water. "Let me be clear, Sam—this story in no way parallels the degree of your trauma in any way, but I think it may answer your question." I paused, again assessing, holding his hand with both of mine, my right hand slithering up to his wrist to catch a pulse for ten seconds. Seven. Good. And it was regular. Even better.

I continued, gazing at the pond, avoiding the distraction of Sam's incredible eyes, "Years ago, driving out of the hospital parking lot after a grueling twelve-hour shift, I hit a squirrel. I heard a thump, looked in the rearview mirror, and saw that the poor thing had a spinal cord injury and was using its front legs to drag the rest of its body to the side of the road. Imagine that, Sam, you get hit by something thousands of times your weight, your cord is severed, and you immediately take what's left of you that works and drag the rest of you to safety. The critter's perseverance and will to live called to me, and as I continued down the road, I got to thinking about its plight and decided to return and put the little rodent out of its misery. When I got to the scene, I pulled over, got the shovel out of my trunk, and planned to beat the living daylights out of that pathetic squirrel, for his own good. I was really upset, not to mention tired, but I recall chuckling at the thought of someone witnessing a menopausal-aged woman beating on a squirrel with a shovel, in scrubs. I'm getting to the point, Sam; hang in there. Well, I couldn't find the poor thing. Gone. It was dusk, and I didn't have a flashlight—I know, I saw your eyes roll. That's awful, right? But I didn't."

Damn, why did I say that? I thought—he had the regret of not having had emergency equipment in the ice accident. I surveyed Sam, head to toe. He looked okay, like maybe he didn't make the connection, a lot of that going around.

Turning my eyes back to the pond, I continued, "Well, as I walked around, and it got darker with each step I slowly took so as not to step on the little varmint, I gave up and headed home. Sam, that night and every night thereafter, for weeks, I woke up in a sweat, with the image of that crawling, dragging damn squirrel in my head, and then I couldn't get back to sleep. I started taking Benadryl at night, but that didn't work. I used my dead mother's long-expired sleeping pills, even doubled up on them. No go. Finally, a full month of very little to no sleep caused me to ask my psych nurse friend for help. She asked me to tell her about the incident. I thought I already had, briefly, but she wanted the long story—everything I could remember about that late afternoon incident. Then, after I told my story, she asked me if I hit a squirrel or a skunk. I had always thought psych people were a bit spacey, but earnestly, I was thinking, hasn't she heard me say squirrel like a hundred times? '*Squirrel*,' I said, *squirrel*, like I was annoyed that she hadn't bothered to listen. And then she shocked me with the news that I had said 'Skunk' four times. She asked if I had any dealings with a skunk lately, and I broke into tears."

After clearing my bangs from my eyes, Sam kissed the tears from my cheeks. Talk about distraction. I would really have to con-centrate to finish the story and I began wondering if he was even listening. I decided to readjust myself on the bench and face him straight on to get both of us back on task. His eyes were aimed at me, but not seeing me, and I wondered if that was because he thought I was comparing his Birch to a squirrel, or even worse, a skunk. In fact, I was. I was in too deep not to finish.

"Okay, so months earlier, Jeff and I had a major skunk problem on our property, and we set a live trap and caught four baby skunks. We didn't know what to do with them, so we took the first suggestion we got from a neighbor and tried to drown them in the river. We were told they would be dead in a few minutes, but after fifteen minutes when we pulled up the trap, the little critters were gasping for breath and Jeff and I both screamed and then cried like babies while we tossed them back and left them there in the river until Jeff retrieved them the next day. We never spoke of the incident then or ever."

I could see the drowning part of my story was very hard on Sam, and I had thought about that when I first planned to share this story with him, in the wee hours of my many how-do-I-tell-this-to-Sam nights. But I decided it was important that he have those reactions, during the day, with someone who loved him—and someone he loved? And someone who knew CPR and who had a charged cell phone in her pocket. I did hurry to end my story, though. "Sam, the point is that, after I cried and talked about the baby skunks with my psych nurse friend, I slept just fine."

I had been holding his hand that lay on my lap, through my whole story, and when I finished, I started rubbing his hand, trying to break his stare that was worryingly locked on the dock. Rubbing with more vigor, I leaned forward and tried to do all I could think of to reign in some eye contact, short of snapping my fingers like a hypnotist. "Maybe, Sam, if you talk about it, how you *felt* and *feel* about it, with your doctor, maybe a psychologist, with me—I hope you can trust me—maybe it will leave your subconscious and stop haunting you at night. Did you know that PTSD has been referred to as a disease of avoidance."

It was minutes of silence before he whispered, "PTSD. Maybe." He appeared thought-filled but composed. I felt good about how he looked, except for the staring. He was blinking, though, albeit barely.

We sat quietly for several more minutes (so not me) still holding hands, Sam still staring at the dock, me staring at Sam, and then I said, "Sam, come home with me. I'll keep you safe at night." My voice was shaking in tandem with my intestines. Did I just propose?

Sam broke his stare for an instant and glanced at me like he was making sure it was me who just said what he thought he had heard, and then he stared away again, but this time he locked his eyes on the ground. After thinking for a long time, long enough for me to entertain doubts about what I had just said, Sam turned and hugged me, our faces cheek to cheek, designedly, I thought, to prevent eye contact, and he said, "Joni, it wouldn't be about keeping *me* safe; it would be about keeping *you* safe." He paused and stretched his neck back, locking my head onto his chest, and with my ear against his fast beating heart, I then heard, "Maybe, if I didn't love you."

Now there does not get a lamer and more backdoor way to say "I love you" than that. Am I right? Even my dear sweet lo-emo Jeff would have known better.

Come to think of it, why didn't you tell him that, Jeff? Isn't that like your job now?

And so, a few dozen lub dubs later, my heart rate now in perfect sync with his, I slowly pulled my head from Sam's chest and looked into those baby hazels, having decided I was not going to respond to his answer—I was going to respond to his delivery. "If you didn't love me, Sam? Is that how I will have to remember you first told me that you loved me? By turning me down?" I wasn't smiling.

He looked like a deer who remembered those headlights, like he had a history of screwing up the important moments in life, perhaps especially with women. When his eyes returned from under his lids, and he again did that headshaking erasure move, he dropped his head like he was lynched and said, "How do I do this? Why do I do this?" This was not a cribbage game where he was the master, in total control of the match. After composing himself, he attempted eye contact, but only briefly as he said, "I have said it to you so many times in my head, Joni, I think I just came to believe I said it aloud to you." And then he snuck a peek, to check if that took.

And it did. Sort of. I didn't like the "it" reference, but I liked the sentiment. "Nice recovery, Dutch. Could you try again without the 'if I didn't' prefix?"

And then he said *it*. And then we kissed—lips, not cheeks. Now if you had told me a dozen or more years ago to imagine two people kissing, the sum of whose ages added to more than 140 years, or as Angie would have said, "The square root of 19,600" (God give her soul exponential joy), I would probably have said, or at least felt, "Yuck." But the Angies of the Borealis world, not to mention lingering loneliness, had caused me to see Sam and I differently.

So, imagine, I had never really kissed an old man, just pecked. So, imagine, too, I had never been kissed by a man when I was old (I noticed I was getting better at saying that I was what I just said I said I was). Baby steps.

What was *that* kiss like, anyone with body parts that still worked well enough to wonder might wonder. Damn sweet, damn smooth, like caramel to a person without cavities or dentures. The supple longitudinal grooves above and below our lips, marks left from our years of past kisses, seemed to fit like tongue and groove, making a smooth soft seal that felt, well, right . . . and satisfying. Who knew? Of course, gerontologists would claim a different cause of those grooves, but what do they know? They don't even know why we age. Free radicals are their best shot.

I admit I did not get that urgent, tingly feeling, obsessed with needing to get to the next step, that next leap, as I did in my earliest days of passionate kissing. Instead, it was more of an overall warmth that I was content to bask in for as long as our joints could tolerate the off-center embrace. And, another plus: the bedamning dryness of senescence came in quite comfy when the adolescent slobber was finally absent during the exchange.

When we eventually peeled back away from each other, and I could see that he enjoyed our first real kiss as much as I had, I came back to the original question that sparked those firsts, that word "no" forever going down like vinegar for me.

"Well, so, let me get this straight, Dutch. The only way you would come home to live with me is if you didn't love me. As in, I can be your lover, but not your caretaker?"

He didn't take long before he said, "I guess that sums it up. I'm sorry, Joni. I've ruined enough lives."

I am hot again, and I am not referring to that short-lived feeling of warmth I just described. "Sums it up"—Angie and Andy would have loved that line. And a line it was, a trite line that Sam was using to put a threshold on our relationship.

I pounced on his assertion like a puppy on a Swiffer, "Oh, for god's sake, Sam, why don't you just take a knee in protest of yourself and be done with this guilt trip? Admit it—you are at Borealis because you need to be punished. You need to suffer. Am I part of that suffering, Sam, as in does it hurt for you to be with me? Because if I'm not, how dare you enjoy my company? How dare you love again? You have penance to serve, damn it. Get on with it!" My hands flew in the air like I was signaling for an ovation. "Oh, that's right, you *have* gotten on with it—congratulations, Mr. Simon, you've just figured out the fifty-*first* way to leave your lover .. Refuse to be rescued from where you have no more a need to be than I did. More pain, more gain, eh Sam? Well, news flash, Mr. Jonathan of Arc, you just ruined life number three!"

Shit, where did that come from? I was trembling like when I woke to find Jeff dead in our bed, on the very morning we were supposed to leave for a fly-in fishing trip to Canada. Sam looked resigned, like he really had just ruined life number three—and counting. I was miserably unclear as to which of us I felt sorrier for.

As I stomped back to my car, no longer needing to shuffle like I belonged at Borealis, all I could think about was that people who said what I just said to Sam should have fast passes to Disney hell. I quaked myself to no sleep that night. And if I took all my life's nights wherein I tossed and turned over pain caused by my whetted tongue, and lined them up one after another, they would not have matched the long-lasting torment of that regret-laden night.

* * *

I spent the next day wondering what to do. Now, years later, this seems quite sick, as in disturbed, but during my restless night it occurred to me that I might be able to capitalize on Sam's martyrdom to get out of the mess I had created. In fact, I was hoping that maybe that was already in the works after my "life number three" shot. I knew I had to say I was sorry, which was not a problem because I was. But I had to be sure he would accept the apology, or he just might call it quits. Unlike with Jeff, I had no reference for how far this teetering man could be pushed or pulled—like playing Jenga, and I hate that game.

The sick part was that I was willing to accept Sam's sense of guilt and obligation, the seeds of which I had planted with my laser tongue, in place of his free-will decision to leave Borealis and come home with me. Yes, I was willing to sacrifice my pride and dignity and succumb to emotionally dragging Sam out of Borealis. And the fact that I hadn't really given much thought to that sacrifice probably meant I had lost all sense of those values, at least for that moment in time.

In my hurting head, I kept singing, "Make a new plan, Stan," hoping to jump-start the creatively manipulative side of my brain. Nothing was coming. Conniver's block. Perhaps my mind would not let me plot against my values? Conscience? I had never quite fully understood this concept, but maybe that was because I did not comprehend its full breadth, for there I was, fully willing, consciously aware, to do whatever I needed to do to get Sam to come home with me, yet the queen of connivance was coming up empty. That explained, I felt like I'd be willing to sell my conscience to the devil, cheap, if the offer were made, to get Sam.

But luckily I did not have to go that devil route. By mid-afternoon the following day, about the time I should have been losing to Sam at cribbage, way after the time I should have been dressed and groomed, Sam showed up at my door with a "Sorry I didn't call first, but I was afraid you'd say not to come" on his lips.

I let him in and uttered a cry of relief as I stated, "Sam, I didn't have anyone to get dressed for. Now that I do, give me a few." He looked worse than I did, tired, like he hadn't slept, like I had hurt him as much as I had worried I did. Clean teeth, pits, pubes, and clothes later, I emerged like a kid playing hide and seek, not even sure where he was, having rudely just left him at the door. *Oh no, did he leave?* "Sam?"

"Here," he said from the dining room table. He looked like he was waiting to be interviewed for a job, sitting at the table, hands folded, dressed impeccably, nervously adjusting things that didn't need adjusting and wouldn't matter if they did. I sat down cross corner from a rare-to-be-seen-in-daylight fidgety Dutch.

"Joni, you don't have to apologize. I trust that you're sorry. What I want to make sure you know is that I am truly sorry that I cannot accept your generous invitation."

No one had ever preempted my apology before. I wasn't sure how to take that. I guessed that I would have been irate if I hadn't been sorry, but being that I was, I thought that must be his point—he trusted me well enough to know that I wasn't really the bitch I had acted like less than forty eight hours ago. But then again, I thought, this was really driving home the fact that I was bitchy beyond apologetic doubt. I was back to not being sure how to take that, and back to reckoning with that palate-busting taste of "no."

My heart, again, was beating so fast that I thought my Fitbit would self-destruct, or that I would. I worried that Sam's was too; could that myocardial muscle of his afford the strain? I looked him over closely, rummaging through my nursing brain for all those skills I might use to conjure another distant assessment. In short time, I decided that if his heart survived our last conversation, it could take anything I could ever dish out.

"I still don't understand your refusal." I was trying very hard to be the person he apologized for.

Placatingly, tossing out an obviously rehearsed reply: "I can understand that," and I suddenly understood what must have been Jane's frustration. He continued, carefully, like he was reading from a teleprompter that he didn't trust, "Look, Joni, you called me a martyr. I am all of that. But martyrs were not bad people. They died for something they believed in. And I am willing to risk my spirit in these final years for the belief I have that I was responsible for the situation Tammy is in today, which is being the sole person to take care of me in my final frail years. Had I been more responsible—and let's be honest here—it wasn't a complete accident. I missed signs about bad ice. I did not have the proper safety equipment. Had that been the case, Tammy would probably be among a group of three dealing with me during my decline. So, Ace, I am at Borealis to ease the burden I created. And I am not very unhappy there." He paused and checked for my reaction, and I was trying hard to display none worth calculating. Coming up short on his take, he finished, "I made this decision when Jane died—that I would move into an assisted living facility when I turned seventy-five, regardless of whether I needed it or not, because I figured I might not be able to know when I needed to come to Borealis, if and when my judgment was to decline."

It was a lot to take in, so, as usual, I focused on a word or phrase. "'Probably', Sam? Probably there would be three, you say. That's a pretty uncertain word to hang the rest of your life on."

"Probably," the corners of his mouth effecting a restrained grin, and added, "but it feels right to me." His verbal and nonverbal package was really pissing me off.

"Well, that's good," my sarcasm slithered back from down deep under to just below skin level, "as long as it's right for you. And tell me, Sam, do I have a sign on me that reads 'Bad ice'?" And, oh my gosh, what an incredibly insensitive metaphor for me to use in this case, but that's the way he looked to me, like I was to be avoided, like I was the fly in his guilt salve.

He inhaled like he was planning to go underwater to retrieve a valuable, and then slowly released these words: "I am older than you, Joni, and I have had a heart attack. And I'm male. Do the math. And pardon me, but you also made a decision to be at Borealis because it was right for you." He nearly ducked.

"Cheap shot, Sam; shame on you. Yes, for six months, and I decided that before I fell in love with you. But now that I think of it, we *are* parental mirror images. You left your family and came here to not hurt them, and I left my family and came here even though I knew it would likely hurt them. Maybe not such a cheap shot after all, about my being your bad ice, eh? Maybe I'm just not good enough for you."

It was the first time I saw him angry. His temporal arteries were bulging, his face was red, and his jugulars dilated to the diameter of a jump rope. He got up and paced the length of the table and back, in total silence, for somewhere in the range of the square root of forty-nine times. Finally, flat-veined and pink-faced, he tried, "Joni, I love you. You left me, not the other way around. What if I asked you to stay? Think about that—what if I asked you to stay with me at Borealis?"

Like an ice water facial—damn him, this man I loved—he had me. In two sentences he made me understand that he could no more leave Borealis than I could stay.

"So what does this mean? We say goodbye?"

He snickered, "Borealis isn't a prison, Ace. At least I don't think it is. Why can't we visit each other? I'm keeping my car at Borealis."

A car? Wow, I thought. That added a twist, had the sound of a game changer. Borealis did not prohibit cars and driving. How could they? But they discouraged it, in large part, I thought, because they did not want to tempt residents who probably should not drive. They also charged a deterring $100 per month parking fee for a space at the far end of their lot, and that area was not plowed in the winter.

"Well, you won't be driving once it snows," I reminded him.

"We can make it work. I am on good terms with Roger. I bet a six-pack would plow me out of that lot."

At that point, our conversation had boiled down to two people in love who were deciding whether to live together or not. I didn't answer because I didn't know what to say—yet again more new territory for me.

And I still liked my idea better.

He then added, "If I can be so bold as to say this, Joni, I think you do not like the idea of dating someone who lives in an assisted living facility." Still standing, he had moved behind me and massaged my shoulders as he said that. And, I knew he was right. Damn, he was so right.

Making Amends Meet

Andy called and asked to meet me for lunch, at a restaurant. I didn't understand the restaurant setting—maybe a change of venue from our last wintry encounter? Of course, I said yes. It would just be him and I, he was careful to inform me.

He picked a quiet time, post lunch, and a quiet restaurant, so quiet that we were their only customers. I wondered about the likelihood of Andy calculating that in his plan. My anxious mind made spam out of that.

I arrived before Andy and chose a table next to the aquarium, hoping the gliding and bubbling would soothe the wait, and that eventually the white noise would drown out our conversation in that all-too-quiet establishment.

Andy came directly to me and kissed me on the cheek with a "Hi, Mom," like nothing had happened between us. *Like nothing had happened*—oh, how I wished. On the backs of that greeting-as-usual, we both slid smoothly into pleasantries, ping-ponging banalities: "How's Ruth?" "How have you been Mom?" "The kids?" "Was everything okay with the house?" But harshly no back at me about *my* latest avocation. At that moment, the thought of whether Andy and Bonnie would have had similar reactions to Jeff if he had been the one who deceived them put a halt to my pong. I drifted off into wonderment of what role, if any, gender or perhaps motherhood, played in all of this. A professional man who decided to do under-cover research to contribute to his profession—would Jeff be sitting here hoping that this meeting was not goodbye?

"Mom?" Andy brought me back. "So, what have you been up to since you are home?" In print that sounds good, like I should not be worried about this being goodbye, but if you knew Andy and heard his tone, you would understand why I thought the jury was still out on me. The best I can do is that he sounded like a parent who comes home to a tranquil, seemingly intact home that had been solely occu-pied for several hours by an untrustworthy child.

I have never been in the mindset of placing in order that which I highly value in life, especially when it comes to people and relation-ships, which are so apples and oranges. But for the sake of my point, here, I will. It seemed so odd to me that the second closest persons in my life (who had occupied first place since Jeff died) did not even know that the first closest existed. I so wanted to share Sam with Andy. But I also sensed that then and there was not the right time nor the right place. I had to navigate around selfish.

And then there was dealing with the guilt of ranking Sam ahead of my children. When Jeff lived with me in the flesh, I always told myself that all three were tied for first, and if I had to order them, like my friends and I once attempted to do over a magnum of wine, I would say Jeff came first. Two of us picked our husbands first, and the third picked her children, and knowing all concerned, that seemed about right at the time, wine notwithstanding. But this was different—chronologically speaking, they should have occupied a commanding lead. And, of course, in terms of invested time and memories, shoo-ins. So why did I feel differently? Was it intensity I was comparing and not degree? Was it that Sam needed me more and, being service-oriented, I confused that with *love*? Hell, if the world could put a shitload of people on the moon, why can't some-one come up with a concrete definition for that word?

After we ordered, Andy took advantage of the break from our waitress to say, "Mom, I accept your apology." I had been hearing that a lot lately, but this acceptance was not a preemption because I had said I was sorry to him and Bonnie when I broke my news to them weeks ago. In my desperation to determine where exactly I stood with Andy, I wondered, right then and there, for the first time in my long life of apologies, whether "I accept your apology" was the equivalent of "I forgive you." I came up with, at that moment, not.

I replied, "Thank you," with the tentativeness of leaving room for a "But." Hearing none, I added, "That's it?"

"That's it," he affirmed. Then, picking up on my fear-filled non-verbal cues that told him I was needing the door-closing sound of "That's it" to be further clarified, he compassionately and promptly followed with, "I mean that's all I wanted to say."

"Well, that's nice of you, Andy, and I know I have a lot of nerve bringing up my needs, but I need more." Makes one wonder why he ever called.

Andy understood me. I did not have to add a lot of fluff around my messaging like I did with Bonnie. "Okay, let's see. How about I tell you what got me to the point where I could bring myself to have this conversation."

"That'll work," I said sadly, and then I risked a weak wink.

"Mom, when I wanted to expand my business, you, and Dad were not fans of that idea, at all, because of the risks, and you told me so, and then I expanded anyway, and then you supported the hell out of me. You saw it was important to me and you changed course. Well, I see some parallels here."

I waited for him to catch his breath because he had said all those words relying on one long lung-exploding inspiration. I found his eyes and asked in a near whisper, "So, are we good?"

He flinched, like it might have been too soon for that question, like it stung, and replied, "Mom, I was really worried about you." A deep sigh later, "I wouldn't say *good* yet, maybe just leave it that we *are*."

I smiled an Andy-made-me-smile smile, and said, "Fair enough. And your sister?"

He brotherly snickered, "I'm afraid she's stuck on the 'I' in her sentence." He knew her so well.

"Can you help me with her?"

"Have I ever been good at that? Really? Has anyone ever been good at that? She feels betrayed, Mom, and that's huge for her, huge for anyone, and especially huge for someone stuck on 'I.'"

At the mention of betrayal, I reflexively looked down at my hands, half-expecting to see them overflowing with thirty pieces of silver. "Well, let's just say I would appreciate anything you can do to help, should you see an opening."

He shook his head in agreement and with spot-on perception ended that conversation just as our waitress was pulling our lunches off the serving counter. "It won't be an opening, Mom, it will be more of a hairline *crack*. But one more thing, Mom," he said as he looked at the approaching waitress juggling my plate and his soup bowl, "I still love you."

There was so much message packed in that one word "still." Andy's "still" meant he loved me before this moment, which I already knew, but I didn't think he had ever said it aloud, save for the "Love you" that stood in for "Goodbye" in our phone conversations. And "still" also meant that he felt I had put my toes to that line that should never be crossed, that in fact so close were my toes to that line that he was refereeing the photo finish. Andy always could pack a lot of Andy into just a few words.

Then, with his steaming chicken noodle soup descending in front of him, he looked up at me, and I noticed his eyes were welled with tears that would eventually absorb or evaporate but never fall—an observation privy only to me, and those gliding fish.

* * *

Within a week of my visit with Andy, I decided to attempt the making of headway with my daughter. I called Bonnie and asked if I could take her three children to a play for which I had already bought tickets—*Pinocchio*, play on play intended. I thought the theme of the play just might force the crack Andy had talked about, the crack I needed—how could she hold back a shot? That, and I had some repair work to do with my grandchildren related to the seventh commandment.

From this invitation came the rare experience of Bonnie being rendered speechless. She had been allowing Laura to communicate with me on Facebook, so I knew there was a good chance Pinocchio would fly.

After a long silence well, long for Bonnie—came, "I guess," with about as much enthusiasm as one agrees to an appointment for a root canal.

I didn't complain about her tone as would be natural for me. "Great. I'll pick them up at five and we can grab a bite before the play?"

An overcast "Yep" hung in the phone, stifling my goodbye.

When I picked up the children, Gordy was there for the hand-off. He was Gordy as usual—cordial, jittery, distant. I wondered if he had been assigned post-play reception duty as well. I decided to play my hand like I had the cards. "Will Bonnie be home when I drop the nippers off? I was hoping to get a chance to see her."

"Uhm, not sure. I mean, I'm not sure when she'll be home." His lack of eye contact coupled with a dramatic clearing of his throat told me the hand-off duty was the vintage head-in-the-sand Bonnie I had suspected it was, and that she was somewhere in audible range.

"Oh, I see," I said, my tone telling him neither of them was fooling me. "Well, can't blame a mom for hoping."

Gordy focused on the children and told them to be good and have a good time. and as I drove away I could almost smell the smoke I knew must have been billowing from their patio, next to a cold grill.

When I returned the children home some five hours later, Bonnie was in their living room when the children ran into the house. She was sitting on their recliner with her back to the door. I called for the children to return and give me a goodbye hug, and as one by one they did, I told each of them I loved them, and then I called out "Goodbye, Bonnie, and I love you, too." My voice splintered on the "too," and that was a good thing, I thought, because it was 100 percent real, and I guessed that she likely noticed. All in all, goal met.

By Thanksgiving, I felt I was back in the fold. Well, maybe that was a bit of a leap and I should be more clear: I was invited to the family Thanksgiving dinner and Bonnie was talking to me, not like she was happy that I was there, but more like she preferred me being there to how unhappy Andy and her children would make her feel if

I wasn't. The good news, I guess, was that during dinner she was not melting any of the whipping cream that topped those pumpkin pies.

In the following months, I worked hard at backing up my apology with virtuous motherly, grandmotherly, and mother-in-law-*ly* behavior. That translated into such activities as watching the nippers whenever asked and offering to watch them even when not, finding the perfect tea set for Meg's birthday, and commissioning Sam to help Gordy get his snow-blower blowing.

The snow-blower fix broke ground for the introduction of Sam. And when Bonnie asked if I wanted to invite him to Christmas, I knew that his place in my heart was beginning to be understood. How could it not be? If they had eyes, they would have to see that I couldn't keep mine off his.

My Christmas present from my children came wrapped that year in the use of humor during our Christmas dinner. No star in the sky marked that divine phenomenon, but it was all of that for me, nonetheless. When passing during our meal, Andy, sitting next to me, offered me the gravy, and when I said "Sure," he shot, "On your beef or in your cup, this year?" And a pause that felt long enough to gestate an elephant was followed by a wave of laughter that eventually even Bonnie surfed upon with an uncontrollable, albeit reluctant grin. And poor Sam looked like he needed to join the children at the kids' table, or get a play book, among all of those "What's so funny?" faces.

We were a family again, laughing together. I understood there was still more reparation to be done, but I also knew that a family that could see humor where there was once adversity was likely to survive.

And bless Andy, or Jeff, or whoever in heaven was responsible for Andy's timely wit.

Sam and I and Joy and Me

Nothing gives kissing an old man a run for its "odd first" status as dating an old man who lives in an assisted living facility. That said, it wasn't as weird as I had imagined.

I visited Sam almost every day during the winter months, weather permitting, because his car was almost always under snow at Borealis and I did not want to contribute to Roger's alcohol problem. I would arrive for our cribbage game, and afterwards I would either stay for dinner or take us out for dinner, again weather deciding. At first, I hated driving home in the dark, but I got used to it after a while. Sam suggested I come earlier, and I just laughed at that notion. What was he thinking? You think you know some old man.

The spring thaw melted more than snow. With Sam driving to my place, we had opportunities for intimacy. It was not so much what I would call making love *to* each other, but rather more like spending our love *on* each other. Hence, where there was once raw convention in our former sex lives, there was parbaked improvisation, and as bad as that probably sounds to one in raw convention mode, I could honestly say there was never a more satisfying experience in my life. It was, also, in fact, a celebration of the one and only non-singular focus activity of old age, that is, the ability to approach sex with a whole body, mind, and spirit, released from the singular genital focus of youth—another "Who knew?"

As our bond strengthened, so did the tendency to compare Jeff and I to Sam and I. Up until then, I had fought that proclivity, out of loyalty to Jeff amidst the percolating fear that he'd come up short. But as time passed, I realized it was not about comparing good and better; it was about comparing a relationship that started with a young couple to a relationship that started with an old couple.

As young lovers, Jeff and I, as I imagine do most young couples, spent much of our time speculating on our future that swirled into the batter of our present, making it nearly impossible to ever live purely in the now. I saw the father of our future children whenever I saw Jeff play with his nephews. I fast-forwarded to us as homeowners when I saw him fix a flat. That is, I saw Jeff through "will-o-bee" lenses—will he be a good husband, good father, good provider, good citizen? Conversely, I saw Sam though "is-o-bee" lenses, because who he—we—would one day be was a big ole fat *if*.

But to be clear about Jeff and me, the future for us was only about a *near* future, for the young would never be caught dead, or more to the point, be caught old, falling off that far-off future cliff. Far into the future is just somewhere the young never go, at least not in our culture.

So different, I pondered, was that aspect of being young and in love compared to Sam's and my late-start relationship, in which the sight of that tunnel's end made the present a much more comfortable place in which to hang out, not to mention more realistic to count on. Second grade math tells an old-start couple that their future will be short. And the decline of their bodies with each breath and step they take tells them that their future will also be wildly unpredictable, as the looming question that surfaces with each sunset, each walk in the woods, each birthday, each Christmas, becomes "How many more?" Show me a couple who looks at a sunset and wonders how many more, and I'll show you an old couple, or a sick young couple.

The good news, I finally found, was that after decades of all those self-helpers telling me to be in the present, in the moment, old age finally gave me a compelling reason to do just that. And it came easy, like never before, the past offering too many regrets for our comfort, and the future, too many risks. I found that to be a very beautiful thing about aging, and as my mom would say, you can take that to the bank.

One afternoon, while rummaging through my third of three "junk drawers," for a pencil sharpener that I knew just had to be in there, I came across a ticket stub from the "World of Color" night-time show at Disneyland that took me back to my trip with Bonnie's family and "Uncle Andy" some years before. I recalled the magnificent dancing lights, over the water, amidst a backdrop of a video of the history of Walt Disney's career of characters. And the song that was blaring on loudspeakers coming from every direction, sending chills down spines and tears down cheeks, was Bob Dylan's "Forever Young," sung by Christina Perri.

Crunching the ticket in my hand, I ran to the television, pulled up Pandora, and typed in a search for "Forever Young sung by Christina Perri." Then I cranked up the volume to an unsafe level. Within seconds I was there, on that beautiful seventy degree starlit evening. I was there, again seeing my grandchildren with their tiny faces aglow, the lightshow dancing in their eyes and highlighting their virgin locks. Then, scanning the crowd, focusing on the many faces and gazing into the very storefronts of their collective minds, I wondered how all those people, young and old, but mainly young, were processing, and at what level, conscious or otherwise, the words of Mr. Dylan's song:

"May your hands always be busy

May your feet always be swift . . .

And may you stay

Forever young."

Searching Dylan online, Wikipedia told me that he was at most thirty-two, most likely busy-handed and swift-footed, when he wrote that song, because it was recorded in 1973 and he was born in '41. The song was written as a blessing to his son, relating his hopes that his child would remain strong and happy. Disney probably liked the verse:

"May your heart always be joyful,

May your song always be sung . . ."

Or perhaps,

"May you build a ladder to the clouds,

And climb on every rung."

Was his song about remaining *young*, or remaining *joyful*? I wondered. Or was it just that at thirty-two or younger, when he wrote the song, those two were one and the same for him? Was it about staying forever young at heart? And if so, what is the difference between a young heart and an old heart that makes so many writers of songs and books and sermons tell us to preserve the former?

I spent considerable time pondering that difference. I thought back to my grandchildren and also the residents at Borealis, and I tried hard to compare their hearts, objectively. I recalled the poem, *Crabbit Old Woman*, which I first read in nursing school in 1974. We students were told that the poem had been written by an old woman in a nursing home, and that it was found among her possessions after the old woman died. One line in the poem took my breath away then and whenever the poem came to mind, for years to come: *There is now a stone where I once had a heart.*"

As I thought of my personal experiences with children, as a mother and grandmother and within the context of what I had learned about them in the three growth and development courses I took over the course of my career, I concluded that a child's heart, while pure and simple, is quite focused on self. That is, if the little nippers were at Borealis, I would not have put them on my "Transformed" list. And well they should not make that list, for they must learn to love themselves before they are able to selflessly love others, which brings about transformation.

When I thought about some of the people on my Borealis "Transformed" list, I found quite the opposite. Sam and Donna were there to spare others. Bert wanted nothing more than to get her family together before she exited. Arnie wanted justice for all. Beyond self, they most certainly were, those old hearts of theirs. Or perhaps better said, those *old at heart*? What's not to want about those hearts? I felt softness, not hardness as from stone. Perhaps the crabbit old woman's reactions were blunted as connections were missed, and those reactions were misinterpreted as a lack of softness? Or, had this crabbit old woman not (yet) transformed? Curious, I decided to look up the history behind the poem and was not surprised to learn that the story we were told about the author of the poem was merely urban legend. That, in fact, the poem was written in 1966 by Phyllis McCormack, a UK nurse, not an old woman who had been living in a nursing home. So, now, that line makes sense to me. The "stone heart" was *not* the perception of an old woman. It was a nurse's perception of an old person or persons. Another caterpillar analyzing the flight plan of a butterfly?

Furthermore, I now see contradiction in the message of the poem. The old woman begs us: *So, open your eyes, nurse…look closer, see me,* and then she describes her life as rich with love: *And I think of the years and the love I have known.* Yet, the author's perception of the old woman's heart is that it is hard as stone. These two images— rich with love and heart of stone—are juxtaposed in my mind. Did the nurse see an ordinary hard stone while missing a *gem*? Was this woman her Charlotte or her Bert *before* … ? I contend it is quite possible that this nurse was seeing herself and not the old woman; that she was seeing what she *perceived* about the hearts of the old at the very time in her life that she was fearing her own approaching *oldness.* I could genuinely relate.

And as I connected to Phyllis McCormack, my thoughts turned back to Mr. Dylan and I wondered what he would say about remaining forever young now that he is old, about my belief that aging successfully at *any* developmental level consists of searching for the joy within each new progression. Like a squirming puppy who scratches and nips and finally settles in a strange human's embrace, we also are fighting old age, only to find that maybe it isn't so bad after all.

In fact, right from the get-go, we human pups are squirming as we first enter our world—not wanting to move on developmentally, needing to be muscled out by contractions, and sometimes even forceps, against our mighty wills. Likewise, other than *longing* to turn sixteen to drive, we generally tend to feel discomfort when leaving each developmental level for the next. And we start bucking the final level way ahead of time, I imagine, because it is our last and the most difficult to predict and, moreover, because we have been led to believe that it is to be avoided, at all cost.

As I looked back at my original reason for my project, it had been to discover a better way to be with the old, better than we had been with Charlotte and others. But that encounter was never about how we did or did not see Charlotte, I finally grasped. It was about how we did or did not see our old selves in our futures. How much clearer could that have been when right there in front of my nose I saw my face in hers, yet I chose, even after that obvious sign, to see the situation as something I could control from outside our combined professional selves, a make-over when it really was a make-under? And with that truth staring me in my Charlotte face, I fear to think about whether, then, was all of what I had done necessary? Or, perhaps, did I need to go through this to finally understand?

Finding joy—it deserved a deeper think. The joy part was easy to understand, but the finding part required some decoding. I looked up the word "find" and read "discover or perceive by chance or unexpectedly." One would think that by one's seventh decade of life, a person would not have to look up a word that is on the "First 300" sight word list for beginning readers. Say, "Right?" But look up I did, for my thought process needed a jump-start.

Contemplating this definition, I came to realize that I had not been *finding* joy during my lifetime; I was passively letting joy find me. Well, not completely passively—I did indeed search out select experiences that I anticipated would *bring me* joy, such as getting married, having children, pursuing a career in something I loved, walking in the woods, treasuring a scale that tilted to my benefit. But discovering joy where it is not apparent, expected, or even likely to be—no. Did I ever do that?

I scanned my memory for evidence of any such discoveries, and I came up with only this example. Jeff and I were on our way to an NCAA basketball championship game, a game in which Andy would be a starter, as a freshman, when we blew a tie rod. We were towed to a very small, rudimentary mechanic shop in a very small, rudimentary town, if it even was a town. At Cal's We Fix It, no one was moving fast. No one looked like they ever moved fast. We were told our vehicle was "next after Shorty's pickup," like we knew Shorty.

Frustration was turning into agitation. They seemed unmoved by our story about not wanting to miss our son's important game. I glanced at Shorty's pickup and was about to ask if Shorty needed his pickup for anything special today, like maybe to visit his dying mother or to donate a kidney, when Jeff read my mind and said, "Don't." I saw his point and acquiesced, for about fifteen minutes, and then I was up again, popping my head through a crack in a door that read, "Employees Only," calling out "Cal?"

The three mechanics, all looking very related with long scraggly brown locks reaching past their eyes, raised their heads from under the hood of the pickup in sync, looking stunned. Even the grease stains on their overalls matched. I reasoned that perhaps their collective dumbfounded reaction was in response to a stranger having breached the "Employees Only" sign, but then the oldest one, close to my age, responded, "He's dead." It was my turn to be stunned. I retreated from the crack like a bird in a clock and caught Jeff's nonverbal cues that conveyed, "Are you satisfied?"

I wasn't. I continued to pop in asking "How much longer?" like a preschooler on a long road trip. I had the idea that this mantra might spur movement. It did not.

Eventually even docile Jeff began showing signs of becoming perturbed and that funded my efforts to pop in every *five* minutes. I swore they were moving slower, hearing less activity as we tapped and paced and paged through *Time* magazines that dated back to Jimmy and Rosalynn.

My pulse doubled. And then, as is usual when I am stressed, it started missing beats. My blood pressure was registering in my right temple like Morse code. Thank God my bladder called. Through a door wearing a handwritten cardboard label, "Ladies," I entered cautiously. Just inside the doorway, searching for a rationale to proceed, I first noticed a urinal that was studded with dead flies. A mirror that hung by one screw was covered with a grey film, allowing reflection of only half my face. In that clouded glass I saw my right eye twitching feverishly, scaring me into taking deep breaths even though aware that I was not in the ideal venue for that therapeutic intervention. As I looked again in the mirror, tilting right to max my reflection, I said aloud to myself, in that filthy lavatory, "You could make this fun." I had no idea where that came from. Then I left the ladies' room with a prayer on my lips for the immune system required to ward off the communicable disease I was certain I was packing.

In the waiting room, I told Jeff that I was going to walk to the coffee shop we had noticed during our tow, a half-mile away, which advertised home-made donuts. "You're hungry?" he asked, surprised because we had lunch just before we broke down. "No. I am in search of fun." He ignored my comment and kept picking at the dried mud on his shoes, with a pen, flipping the little mud scraps onto a brittle sun-yellowed real estate flyer that he had carefully spread on the grimy floor. *So Jeff.*

On my way back, toting donuts that were damn heavy, I passed our van, which remained where the tow truck had left it, and grabbed our box of cassettes—and that tells you how long ago I last remember myself making joy. I had noticed a boombox in the workshop during one of my preschooler pop-in moments.

Unnoticed by the crew of three, this time I completely defied the "Employees Only" sign and actually entered the shop which made the ladies' restroom look like a spa. After snapping a Beach Boys tape into their boombox, I hoisted myself up and onto the greasy counter, cranked the volume up to ten, held out the open box of donuts, and yelled, "Break time" above "Fun, fun, fun." They came running towards me like I had yelled "Treats" to a pack of dogs who knew what the word meant. They started chomping on donuts that may have been made at home, but not any time recently. The oldest mechanic was suggesting rhythm, so I hopped off the counter and grabbed his hand for a jitterbug around the room, both of us kicking aside tools, rags, and age-old candy bar wrappers, to the beat.

Jeff even risked breaching the "Employees Only" sign, a real challenge for the ultimate rule follower that he was. I had fun. They had fun. Jeff had fun, mostly watching us. Joy! I found it! Correction—I believe I made it!

We missed the game and I didn't care, because I believed we would have missed it anyway, fun or no fun. Truth was, I almost hated to leave those guys, and they acted like they felt the same about us. And why that epiphany of the self's ability to turn sand into gold did not change my life right then and there, I still wonder, for that was amazing power. Perhaps this inability to transform at this point can best explained by the saying, "When the student is ready, the teacher will come." I was not completely ready, and so I saw it as useful within the confines of that situation only. How my life could have changed had I recognized the potential in this power? Perhaps, on occasion, I relied on this cream? Either way, the experience was tucked away in my grey matter, for future reference, when I was ready. When I was older? When I was old?

And when our son's coach heard about our tie rod incident, he invited us to the team's review session of the game video. "A first," so Andy informed us. More cream. More joy, especially because the game was a win.

As I now recall this long-ago occurrence, I think about my likely future at some Borealis or beyond Borealis place, places where joy finding me, as it had so dutifully done for me for so many decades, would then be in short supply. And if it couldn't find me, I would be joyless, unless . . . unless I could take what I finally had learned from that tie-rod experience and do that lemonade magic, anticipating mega lemons in those places where joy flowed incognito.

And thus, I decided to practice *making* joy, searching for its ingredients in unlikely places. While brushing my teeth, I took my phone along and played my favorite song, "What a Wonderful World" by Luis Armstrong—joy. But then, at that point I still had all my teeth, so no sorrows yet to deal with there. Mail retrieval—nothing was coming to mind, so I stood at the mailbox and waited for something to present itself. I heard a soft sound. It was a leaf, or a twig, being moved by a garter snake slithering out of its skin among the rocks stacked around the post. I sat crisscross applesauce and did my Sheryl Crow impersonation, air guitaring, and quietly singing, "A Change Could Do You Good." The reptile was aware of my presence: his head reached high and he paused his shedding movements for well over a minute. He then continued, and it took him almost fifteen minutes to complete his wardrobe change. Later it took me seriously into my night's sleep to get past the wonder of how much more of life I had been missing.

As I was lying down to sleep, I told God a knock-knock joke that I made up:

"Knock, knock."

"Who's there?"

"God."

"God who?"

"God if I know but You should; You know everything."

And it was that day, or rather night, feeling joy, that I decided to re-allocate upper case status to my Friend whose fidelity I had doubted in my despair. And I bet He got a kick out of that—the tides of faith reversed.

I felt ready—I could make joy wherever and whenever I decided. I could join the *Incredibles* family, for I possessed a unique super-power, though I could be tempted to swap my power for Elastigirl's, considering the time it had been taking me to get dressed most days.

* * *

Back to Sam and me, perhaps the most amazing self-discovery that occurred surrounding my project was when I found out that accepting "no" could turn out to be a good thing. What a shock to find that I was happy with the way things were with Sam at Borealis and me in my home, without him.

Often during my time alone at home, I would try to picture what it would be like if Sam had taken me up on my offer to come home with me. In the bathroom, I pictured his toothbrush and razor there alongside mine, and that certainly seemed okay, even cozy. Then in the bedroom I looked at my clothes tossed over two chairs and a bed and, thinking about how I'd have to pick those up, I concluded that this would probably be a good thing for me to do anyway. Similarly, when I looked in my refrigerator and thought about how I would need to incorporate Sam's food, I saw that as not so bad either, because at least Sam cooked. But then I eyed that remote and thought about losing that total control—ouch. As I pecked at my laptop, I considered when and where I would find the alone time to write or read, or not so much even the alone time, but the right time, while sharing so much space and time with another who attracted the tart out of me.

Even worse, I thought about how sexy it wouldn't be to see him with his perfect day-hair mussed in the morning or to watch him paint his toes with antifungal tincture and pick the sandman out of his eyes, and I thought, maybe his idea did turn out to be better.

And then there was all of that and more about me, in reverse. I was a real sight in the morning, and since I retired, I had a habit of staying that way until the sun perched on my roof. The way we were, apart, I was always excited to see Sam, but would I be if he lived with me? I was always interested to hear what he had to say, but would I be if he was always there? We would almost always be together, and I had never had that experience with a man. Jeff was dead before we ever retired. And I remembered how, even with Jeff and I, fully immersed in jobs and kids, the excitement had dropped off because eventually we had just plain seen and known too much of, and about, each other. We were comfortable, not excited. Was that bad? No. Not bad. But that was not my question to myself. My question was, was it better?

I liked dating Sam. Why would I want to chance messing that up? And I came to wonder if this was another, or even *the* real, reason he had said no, consciously or not.

I continued writing at night, but by then I had moved from journaling to writing this book. I was moving along quite well at this until one night when I had the gut-wrenching thought: what if no one wants to publish my book? How that likelihood escaped me for almost three decades cannot be explained beyond perhaps my overwhelming drive to tell the story serving to mask all potential obstacles. This new fear left me with a writer's block the likes of which I had theretofore not experienced, except for when Sam was sick and missing in my Borealis life.

What made me think I was any good at telling stories? What made me think I had anything worth writing that anyone would deem worth reading? I had a hard time talking to even myself about this and wanted to, but could not, share it with Sam. He asked often how my writing was coming. All I ever answered was, "Along." I found myself one evening talking to Charlotte, telling her she was the one who inspired all of this. Quite sure that she was dead by then because she was near dead back then, I introduced her to Jeff and asked them to team up and get me through this jilt of confidence. Weeks later, I decided heaven must be devoid of social media, because the two of them did not appear to connect, for my benefit at least.

My sleep had been dwindling in direct correlation with my confidence, or was it coming to be the other way around? I did not know. And then while I sat idly at my computer one afternoon, a squirrel scurried across the screen of the window I was facing, jump-starting me like an AED into saying aloud, "Tell Sam!"

Slumber then gradually waxed as steadily as it had waned, but come it did, after many long talks with the person I believed held faith not only in my project, but in me.

And as I plumped my pillow for a good night's sleep, I reflected, maybe Jeff and Charlotte did make friends.

Never Been Good at Higher Power Math

My math was all wrong—I could count cards, but not destinies. I became the caregiver, not the cared-for, as I had predicted. Only a couple years into our love, Joni had a stroke. It was a left-brain stroke, leaving her with right-sided paralysis along with speech, language, and memory problems. She had been doing the final rewrite on this book before submitting it for publication when her brain bled.

When thinking about asking her if she'd come to live with me, at Borealis, after her stroke, at first, I was foretelling that she'd say no, as I once said to her. But then I remembered what she once told me when we were talking about our endings. I had said the thing I feared most was needing to be cared for by someone I love, perhaps because the two people I then loved most were women, and she said she most feared being cared for by someone she didn't love, some-one who didn't love her. I guess maybe she saw too much as a nurse. Anyway, she said yes.

Borealis was good about her coming back. She needed more care than they were able or willing to provide, but I said I would assist for as long as I could and asked if we could just run a day-by-day trial. They said yes, too—perhaps the pint-sized endowment I offered made the "yes" roll off their tongues a bit easier. They gave us adjoining rooms, but we slept in my bed.

She could no longer add, so our days of cribbage were over. But we could play rummy, sort of. She wouldn't stand for me not playing my game and I wouldn't stand for me beating her all the time, so we decided on a handicap for her, and that worked well but only after I promised, on our love, that I wouldn't let up. I knew she secretly thought of rummy as her route back to cribbage.

Neither of us had been avid TV watchers, and Joni struggled with the eye and brain strain of reading. She said her eyes were reading two different parts of the same page. I could not imagine. So, we spent our days mostly with me reading to her or me wheeling her around the halls of Borealis in the winter, and around the lake whenever else we could. We picnicked whenever weather permitted. But winters were long in this northern-lights district, making those hallways qualify for the longest wedding aisle in the history of love.

We did manage to take a short cruise together. We wanted to try it out and see if maybe we could pool our resources and make a deal with a cruise line to live on one of their ships indefinitely, but the waves did nothing to allay my night frights, and, despite those mammoth baffles, they also played havoc with Joni's balance. She fell and broke her wrist on the last day of the cruise.

I felt like I was watching another person I love drown again, only this time in slower motion. When she tried to call me "Dutch," it came out sounding like "Bitch"—her Ds very difficult for her, her Bs not so much—and at first that made her cry, but after I told her I thought it was a Freudian slip, she managed to chuckle, and then I begged her to keep trying.

Once when she became confused about her grandchildren's names, she must have had a flashback to when she had pretended to not know their names during her project days, and she tried to say that it was poetic justice. But when she tried to pronounce "poetic," it came out sounding like "pathetic," and it was all I had to do to not cry along with her, on my outside. She was losing the strength necessary to make joy. I tried to make it for her. Most days I think I might have.

I hired an editor to complete the final rewrite of her book and to market it for publishing. And if you are reading this, she was successful. I never told Joni because after the stroke she never brought-up the book. I imagined that her unpublished work was, for her, what my residence at Borealis has been for me. And I guess we will both just have to wait to see if we get any credit for our efforts at restitution.

I once told her that I never loved a woman more than I loved her, and that was true. More truthful might have been that I loved her more than I had loved anyone, but that was hard for me to say aloud, as I now read it was for her also. That first love loyalty tends to complicate the communication of subsequent loves, if it was a good first love. And our first loves were good for both of us, so we struggled with that, on the outside, but not in our hearts.

What Jane and I had was a marriage. It was a polar attraction of opposites. It wasn't a bad marriage, by any means, and I loved her very much for all the days of our life together. We learned to love each other despite our differences, and because of our children. It was work and worth every effort. Our differences were complementary. They added flavor. We were a stew.

But what Joni and I had was a slow, simmering union of our seasoned minds and hearts that made the separate parts of us nearly unidentifiable as mine versus hers. We were purée. Better? No, different. Effortless. Able to read one another. It was the kind of love I needed at that time in my life, both loves were— symbiotic, like bees and flowers, and I remain forever grateful for that. I read now that Joni wondered about my relationship with God. We did talk about it some but what I never got a chance to tell her was that she was proof for me of God in my life, God on my side, after having wondered for so many years how He could have abandoned our family so.

Truly, there is something very special about a relationship that starts with a tangible, visible end. Every moment becomes special, like the countdown on New Year's Eve when every number carries behind it an exclamation point.

There was only one person of all the people who knew us— family, friends, Borealis staff—who did not ask us if or when we were getting married, and that was Andy. Even Tammy succumbed. After Joni died and I found myself re-reading her Borealis notes just to keep in touch, I added Andy to Joni's "Transformed" list.

We never even talked about marriage even though everyone else did. Joni would probably have said we had transformed past that ceremonial need to commit our lives to one another, and I would have said that such a move in our late stage of life would seem like offering help when the last dish was being washed. That would have been my glib rejoinder. However, the sincere sentiment would have been that it would, by that time, seem to lessen the relationship—like what we had could be better if . . .

And nothing could *ever* have been better.

I often thought about how my grief over losing Birch and Jane had profoundly changed me. I called it grief, but now that Joni is gone from my life, I realize that what I thought was grief was overshadowed by guilt and only now, somehow released from that guilt with Joni's death, I am able to grieve all three. And when I think about how different of a man I was, before my losses of Birch and Jane, I wonder whether Joni would have ever fallen in love with that man. She found me broken and she made me whole again, and I know of no greater love or nurse than that.

Finally, whenever I now re-read her book, I think about her revelation of successfully growing old by forever finding or making joy, and I reminisce that she was all of that for me. I just wished our forever here had been longer. But the joy was always there, from the moment I laid my eyes on her to the moment she closed hers forever, and still.

Charlotte Made Me Do It; Love Made Me Not.

This is a work of non-fiction.

This is a work of fiction.

Charlotte, my patient (I really am a nurse), truly inspired my plan. And there was a plan. But the closer I got to carrying it out, the more I realized I couldn't go through with it, for the sake of my family, for fear of my family, if I am now being totally honest. All those worry prayers in italics were what kept me up nights while planning the project that never materialized. Yet, for all the years between Charlotte, on my forty-fifth birthday, and decades later, the experiences I collected from my patients *did* become the foundation of my story.

That is, the characters portrayed in this story are largely composites of the many patients I encountered while concentrating on the person, and many of these human amalgams were then sampled as case studies in my practice as a nurse educator. I was a nurse educator for the last twenty-five years of my career. I hope that disclosure is not a turn-off for any nurse readers—for the mere thought of a couple of my nursing instructors still gives me a chill. That is why I left this tidbit for the end.

When I elected to forsake Plan A, I decided to spread, like grout, a story around these human mosaics, linking them in these chapters in the hopes of sharing what I had been learning about the old and caring for the old. I found that, during those concentrated watching years, I experienced plenty worth sharing, consoling myself that the ruse probably was unnecessary. And I became a much better caregiver when I shifted my concentration to the person instead of the tasks. *If only I had done that sooner, dear Charlotte.*

By the way, all of us caregivers *say* we do this (concentrate on the person and not the tasks), but most of us do not. Not *really*. Maybe once in a while, perhaps superficially, but not consistently, not deeply. And "beyond task" nursing sadly is all too often limited to the patients we like, not necessarily the person who most needs a nurse—the person for whom anxiety, fear, worry, and pain cause behaviors that are not pleasant to be around.

To be fair, it is not always our fault—patient/staff ratios, documentation requirements, and our own level of wellness are just a few of the many factors influencing the quality and quantity of our time with our patients. But if we are totally honest, we could do better, because it really isn't just about time. I've been there. It isn't. Time is our excuse because it is measurable, whereas commitment, dedication, passion, and the art of achieving oneness with another human's spirit are not.

Confession: in my nurse beginnings, I showed up to work on all too many Sunday mornings dressed in Saturday night's headache and bloodshot eyes. Later, as a young mom, I would show up in much the same condition, only all-nighter teethers and pukers were then to blame. Call in? No, I did not want to use up my PTO time that I would eventually need for what *really* counted. How do I defend my often espoused "privilege of nursing philosophy" with that behavior in my professional past? I can't. I wonder to this day who, or what, I missed—those finer connections, those Berts.

My patients deserved more—they deserved a whole nurse. Tasks are robotic; conversely, focusing on the person is complex, time-consuming, energy-zapping. Not to mention the fact that we nurses are not encouraged or rewarded by our employers to do this. Our documentation and our tasks are reviewed via quality assurance, but our handholding, our listening, our "just being with" are not. This revelation was probably the biggest pearl I discovered during this endeavor.

To be clear, there was no actual "project." There was only a contrived project. Therefore, there was no Borealis in northern Minnesota. There was no Sam. My husband in my real life never died, and his name is Mike. My children are LeeAnne and Robert. And I never had a stroke, nor a mastectomy, and I am (probably) still alive at the date of this publication. The characters in this book are fictitious, except my mom.

But don't think for one moment that I did not earn the license to present loss, for loss and I are no strangers—I know her like a best friend. Moreover, I recognized her in the eyes, sounds, and touch of the personalities I showcased in this story. I recognized her in the persons I was finally able to truly encounter, the persons I most likely would have missed before Charlotte.

Psychologists tell us that loss implies the absence of something that has meaning and value to the person. I would agree. All of us old know loss well, for old is nothing if not loss. As the years roll out, the losses mount—mobility, flexibility, heart, liver, kidney function, vision, hearing, touch, hair, balance, mind, endurance, independence, coping skills, judgement, friends. Aging, in and of itself, is commonly described as a "*loss* of youth." And while the losing is relatively the same for all of us, give or take contributions from genes, environment, and lifestyle, what is very different for each of us is our *take*.

We hear a lot about the old having the plus of wisdom. Okay, I will go with that, sort of. But are we all sitting in our rocking chairs spewing out philosophical gems which others find worth recording and following? Maybe in Hollywood. Maybe in another culture.

As I see it, where the rubber meets the road regarding losses in old age is our relative acceptance of these losses—or not, our relative transforming—or not. And I searched diligently for what makes that difference. Personality? Organic? Learned? The degree or frequency with which the losses occurred? The ability to find and make joy despite these losses? The ability to make joy *out of* these losses?

With no hard-core research to rely on, I could only be certain of what it was for me. What caused me to eventually accept being old and actually embrace it? A searched soul later, I decided, as have many before me, that without loss there can be no gains because nothing would be valuable unless it *could* be lost. And I also decided acceptance had a lot to do with generativity—that is, for those I love to experience fullness in their lives—careers, raising a family, including grandchildren and great-grandchildren—I must move on. I have to drop off life's conveyer belt to make room for those after me. And I started to look forward to seeing that happen once I began moving towards acceptance. That is, I started to make joy out of this end stage when I realized loss was gain, when I realized wisdom meant getting out of the way, handing the baton, in a nice way, in a joyful way. A selfless exit.

I learned that this is what aging successfully is for me—not *staying* active, *staying* youthful, but rather accepting that I am *not staying* and making the best of the time I have left. Ironically, that very realization makes me more active, more youthful, but the mindset is not "to stay." The mindset is to leave graciously, leave the best part of me. And that mindset makes all the difference, and that mindset makes joy for me.

As I review my lists, the thought occurs to me that maybe transforming equates with the willingness and ability to make joy—people who "get it." The Borealis composites surely have become a part of me, as do the spirits of all the persons we have *truly* encountered in our lifetimes. Yes, we caregivers are so privileged to have those opportunities every day of our practice, if we can *see* these encounters for the privileges they afford.

Furthermore, the very nature of my lists tells me that I was drawn to develop characters who represent an active transformation within their developmental stage, accepting their oldness. No, much more than accepting—embracing, perhaps even inviting old age. It now makes sense that this would have been the case because I was searching for that comfort zone myself. They became the me of my future.

I realize that, at this point, some readers might feel manipulated, deceived, "duped." Charlotte would empathize, or, more to my efforts, hopefully readers can now better empathize with Charlotte? Some might also feel relief in finding out that I am not the self-centered bitch you deemed me to be.

In the end, some people claim angels, while some claim devils, made them do it. I claim Charlotte, and I will let you, the reader, decide which, if either, she was.

Thank you for reading my story, and may you remain forever finding and making joy. And Bob Dylan, maybe we can chat someday about "Forever Young," now that we both are old.

It feels good to be good with old age. I admit, however, that, whereas I believe I am good with *being* old, *saying* I am old goes down like calling my mother-in-law "Mom" ever did. Furthermore, *hearing* that I am old, not much better, mainly because I don't always know the labeler's definition of old.

But most sincerely, there is freedom in my good-with-*being*-old feeling. No contractions to struggle against. No squirming puppy. No need to smell like garlic. I try hard to embrace the image that we aging petals will fall to the ground, yet leave behind a memory of a once-upon-a-time amazing display, our life, which will bring forever joy when we grounded petals serve as nourishment for the next generation who will eventually display the best part of us in their own amazing display. We *are* the fertilizer of their lives. And you can take that to the bank.

See you soon, Mom. And Dad and Sis. And God?

"Just drop off the key, Lee . . . and set yourself free."

Joni Bohne (my real name)